CANAL WALK[illegible] ONE

DERBYSHIRE AND NOTTINGHAMSHIRE

BY

JOHN N. MERRILL

MAPS AND PHOTOGRAPHS
BY JOHN N. MERRILL

a J.N.M. PUBLICATION

1986

a J.N.M. PUBLICATION

J.N.M PUBLICATIONS,
WINSTER,
MATLOCK,
DERBYSHIRE.
DE4 2DQ

This book is copyright under the Berne Convention. All rights are reserved. Apart from any fair dealing for the purposes of private study, research, criticism or review, as permitted under the Copyright Act, 1956, no part of this publication may be reproduced, stored in a retrieval system, or transmitted in any other form by any means, electronic, electrical, chemical, mechanical, optical, photocopying, recording or otherwise, without the prior permission of the copyright owner. Enquiries should be addressed to the publishers.

Conceived, edited, typeset and designed by John N. Merrill.

© Text and routes—John N. Merrill 1986

© Maps and photographs—John N. Merrill 1986

First published May 1986

ISBN 0 907496 30X

Typesetting interface work by Steve Rothwell Typesetting Services,
20 St Ann's Square, Manchester M2 7HG.

Typeset in 9½ point on 10½ point Plantin Roman, Italic and Bold

Printed by: Higham Press Ltd., New Street, Shirland, Derbyshire.

ABOUT JOHN N. MERRILL

John combines the characteristics and strength of a mountain climber with the stamina, and athletic capabilities of a marathon runner. In this respect he is unique and has to his credit a whole string of remarkable long walks. He is without question the world's leading marathon walker.

Over the last ten years he has walked more than 55,000 miles and successfully completed ten walks of at least 1,000 miles or more.

His six walks in Britain are—

Hebridean Journey	1,003 miles
Northern Isles Journey	913 miles
Irish Island Journey	1,578 miles
Parkland Journey	2,043 miles
Lands End to John O'Groats	1,608 miles

and in 1978 he became the first person (permanent Guinness Book Of Records entry) to walk the entire coastline of Britain—6,824 miles in ten months.

In Europe he has walked across Austria (712 miles), hiked the Tour of Mont Blanc and GR20 in Corsica as training! In 1982 he walked across Europe—2,806 miles in 107 days—crossing seven countries, the Swiss and French Alps and the complete Pyrennean chain—the hardest and longest mountain walk in Europe.

In America he used the world's longest footpath—The Appalachian Trail (2,200 miles) as a training walk. The following year he walked from Mexico to Canada in record time—118 days for 2,700 miles.

During the summer of 1984, John set off from Virginia Beach on the Atlantic coast, and walked 4,226 miles without a rest day, across the width of America to San Francisco and the Pacific Ocean. This walk is unquestionably his greatest achievement, being, in modern history, the longest, hardest crossing of the USA in the shortest time—under six months (177 days). The direct distance is 2,800 miles.

Between major walks John is out training in his own area —the Peak District National Park. As well as walking in other areas of Britain and in Europe he has been trekking in the Himalayas four times. He lectures extensively and is author of more than sixty books.

EREWASH CANAL

SAWLEY BRIDGE MARINA

CONTENTS

INTRODUCTION

Canals have fascinated me for a long time and for the last three years I have wanted to write a book on the canals of the Peak District and Derbyshire area. I had walked the Cromford Canal often and on, my walk round the Derbyshire boundary, much of the Erewash Canal. In the southern end of the county I had written about Shardlow and a canal walk, several years ago.

At first I outlined a book of fifteen walks but as I began walking them I felt I was not doing justice to the scope available. Whilst it rained or was murky in the Peak, the canals were always clear, calm and almost walker-free! I started with the Cromford Canal before exploring the Erewash Canal. Here I came unstuck, for the more I walked the more I wanted to learn about the 'waterway system of 200 years ago'. I had become hooked and kept 'discovering' canals, such as the Beeston, Nottingham, Nutbrook and Derby. Many were almost lost but their lines still traceable. My fifteen walk book increased to twenty, then twenty-five at the most. Even that was not enough, I would have to do another book—now two more!—and this one has 32 walks in!

In the end I resolved, simply because I enjoy local history but also you can see for yourself where history was made, that I would have to walk each canal from end to end. The Chesterfield Canal is the longest in the book and there is scope for more than the nine walks I have done on it, but I hope they illustrate the variety of walking to be found on it. Obviously there is much more history than I have detailed—each canal really needs a book on its own—but the beauty of canal walking is that you can see and discover for yourself its history.

Whilst the walking is flat it is never dull and you can always return the same way along the canal. However, I have made the walks circular so that you appreciate more of the area and the canal setting. The walks are suitable for everyone and there is a proliferation of inns along the way. I have enjoyed immensley these walks and hope they give you just as much pleasure as you walk and explore the transport routes of yesteryear.

HAPPY WALKING,

John N. Merrill

JOHN N. MERRILL WINSTER. FEBRUARY 1986

TRENT LOCK

JAMES BRINDLEY—*1716-1772*

It is perhaps fitting that the greatest canal engineer of his time should be born in Derbyshire. James Bridley was born at Tunstead near Wormhill (close to Buxton). At Wormhill is a drinking trough to his memory. He was uneducated and could hardly read or write. From an early age he was fascinated by mechanical things. He saw a corn mill and sketched the parts to understand how it worked. At the age of 17 he went to work for a millwright, named Abraham Bennett, at Sutton near Macclesfield. He soon showed a natural talent for designing mechanical works using water. He soon earned himself a nickname—'the schemer' for his now apparent genius. On one occasion he worked at a mill on one of the Duke of Bridgewater's estates.

His skill soon reached the ears of the Duke and began one of the major partnerships in transportation. The Duke needed engineering advice for he wanted to move coal from his mines on the Worsley estate to the port of Manchester. He had devised a canal but was stuck at making locks. Brindley suggested an aquaduct, which was thought unrealistic by the establishment. But the Duke could see it was a good sound idea and it was built—900 yards long and 17 feet high—carrying the canal over the river Irwell at Barton. The canal was opened in 1761 and became the wonder of the year. This immediately reduced the price of coal in Manchester from 17d (7p) a hundredweight to 3 ½d (1½p).

Whilst canals were already being built for short distances, Brindley's expertise launched the country into a fervour of activity, with the next 80 years being the canal's heyday—until the advent of railways. With the Duke he went on to construct 360 miles of canals. His next project was the Manchester—Liverpool canal, 24 miles long. Brindley was poorly paid for work—3s 6d (17½p) a day. The labourers were getting 1s 2d (6p). He went on to link Liverpool, Hull and Bristol together by waterway—The Grand Trunk system.

Others followed such as the Birmingham Canal in 1768, the Droitwich Canal and Chesterfield Canal. Incredibly, Brindley never wrote anything down, he kept everything in his head. He simply went to bed to think it out! He died aged 56, on September 27th 1772.

> *'The Rugged Brindley has little to say for himself.*
> *He has chained the seas together. His ships do visibly float over valleys, and invisibly through the hearts of mountains; the Mersey and the Thames, the Humber and the Severn, have shaken hands.'*
>
> Carlyle.

JAMES BRINDLEY
PLAQUE

CHESTERFIELD CANAL

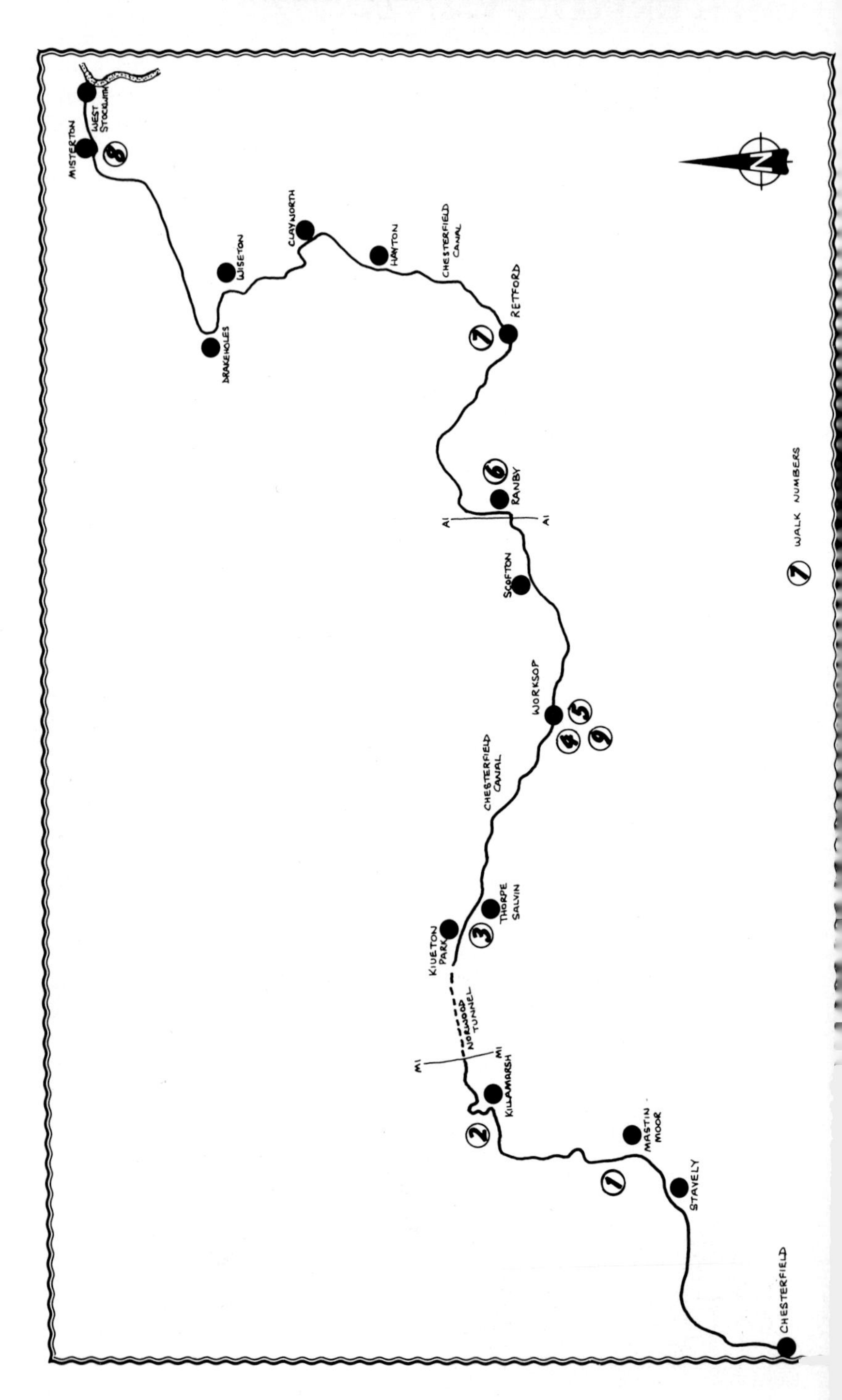

CHESTERFIELD CANAL

A canal from Chesterfield to the Trent was promoted by many local interests. The London Lead Company needed a more efficient way to move lead from their smelt-mill at Ashover. The coal owners of North East Derbyshire and the Cavendishes wth their furnaces at Staveley pressed for a scheme. James Brindley surveyed a proposed line in 1769 but died before it was complete. The Chesterfield Canal Act recieved Royal Assent on March 28th 1771. Little over three years later part of the canal was opened but the construction of the 2,850 yard long Norwood Tunnel delayed the overall opening and was not officially opened until June 4th 1777. The price of coal dramatically dropped at East Retford from 15s 6d (77½p) a ton to 10s 6d (52½p). Originally the canal was expected to cost £100,000 but when completed it had cost £152,000.

The canal was 46 miles long with 65 locks—a major number were at the Chesterfield side of the Norwood Tunnel. There were plans to link the canal with Sheffield, Derby and the north west, but nothing was done, partly because of the terrain to be encountered. There were two tunnels; the Norwood which proved to be a major engineering undertaking for its time, and Drakeholes tunnel—154 yards long. Between Retford and West Stockwith the canal was wide to take sailing barges, hence the Placket Inns. The rest was much narrower as can be seen by the locks remains at Norwood. Horse drawn boats travelled at 3 m.p.h. and the return journey from Retford to West Stockwith took 10 hours.

At first the canal was very successful with the cargo being predominantly coal, but corn, lead, bricks, stone and general goods were also shipped. Up to 1836 the canal company paid out dividends of between 5%—8%. In 1848, 200,000 tons were shipped; ten years later it had dropped to 110,000 tons.From 1888 it was running at a loss, and like all canals could not compete with the cheaper and faster rail system. The Norwood tunnel was constantly needing attention, suffering from subsidence and roof collapses, which proved too costly in the end. In 1908 it was closed for good and the section to Chesterfield became abandoned. The section from Worksop to the Trent was still in use and in 1939 only 40 boats worked the canal carrying 20,000 tons per annum still being horse drawn. By 1955 canal traffic had ceased with the closure of the Walkeringham brickworks.

Today the section from Worksop to the Trent is navigable and popular during the summer and largely saved by voluntary working parties. The section from Worksop to Kiveton Park is water filled and popular with fishermen, with some really unspoilt walking around Kiveton Park/Thorpe Salvin area. The section from Norwood to Chesterfield is at first water filled but soon becomes just a basic line to Chesterfield, which can still be followed along a right of way.

CHESTERFIELD CANAL, NEAR HAYTON

CHESTERFIELD CANAL—WALK 1—SPINKHILL—*5 miles*

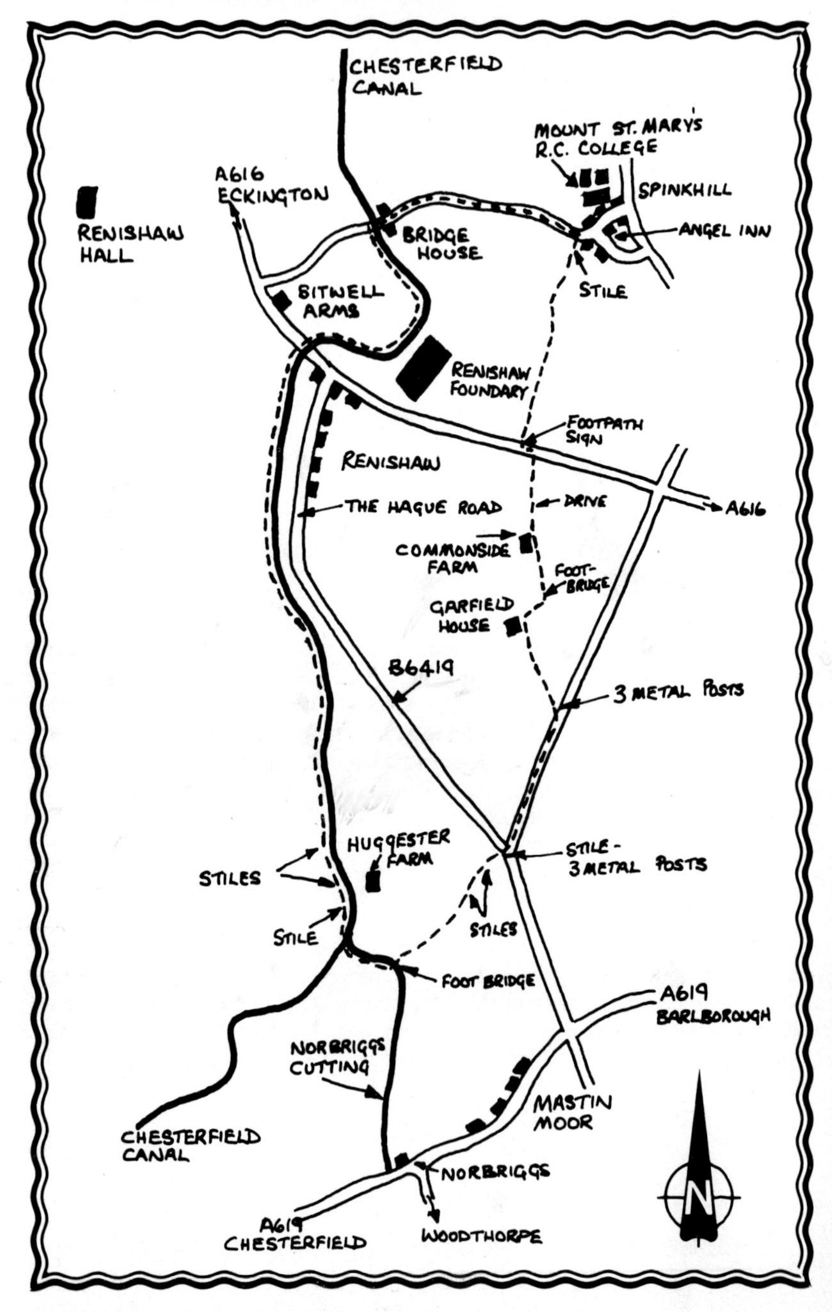

SPINKHILL—much of the village consists of Mount St Mary's College. The church, whose spire is a famous landmark, was built in 1845 and designed by John Hansom, famous for the Hansom cab.

CHESTERFIELD CANAL—WALK 1—
5 miles—*allow 2½ hours*

ROUTE—*Spinkhill—Emmett Carr—Commonside Farm—Garfield House—Happy Valley—Norbriggs Cutting—Chesterfield Canal—Bridge House—Spinkhill.*

MAPS—*1:50,000 Sheet No 120—Mansfield and The Dukeries —1:25,000 Sheet No SK 47/57—Worksop (South) & Stavely*

CAR PARK—*no official car park.*

ABOUT THE WALK—You start from Spinkhill and appreciate the Chesterfield Canal's location in the valley below.First you descend and cross fields to reach Norbriggs Cutting, an arm of the canal. Shortly afterwards you follow the line of the canal for nearly 3 miles tracing its route around Renishaw. A short ascent returns to Spinkhill.

WALKING INSTRUCTIONS—From the Angel Inn in Spinkhill walk south westerly along the road to Top Farm, 20 yards away and turn left at the road's righthand bend, onto a track. A few yards later is the stile and path beside the hedge on your right. After 150 yards bear left (now heading due south) and follow the well defined path away from the hedge and begin descending to the A616 road ¼ mile away. On your right is Renishaw Foundry. Ascend the steps to the road and path sign. Turn left then right onto the drive to Commonside Farm. Pass the farm on its left and continue on the path as you descend to a stream and footbridge. Cross this and ascend to another drive. Turn right along this, ignoring the right turn and just before the entrance to Garfield House, turn left into a hedged path. Follow this, soon keeping the field boundary on your left to a minor road. Turn right and a little over ¼ mile later at the road junction—Mastin Moor/Renishaw road—cross over to the three metal posts stile.Descend to a stile then another with Happy Valley farm on your right. Cross the track to another stile and follow the field boundary to another stile. At the end of the next field reach a footbridge over Norbriggs Cutting.

Turn right and follow the path beside the disused canal to its junction with the Chesterfield Canal.This canal is completely filled in and only the path line indicates its route. Turn right and follow the canal line for 2½ miles. First it is open country before entering woodland near Renishaw. After passing under the A616 road the canal turns right past Renishaw Foundry on your right, before swinging left to Bridge House and the Spinkhill road. Turn right at the road and walk up it to Spinkhill and the Angel Inn ½ mile away.

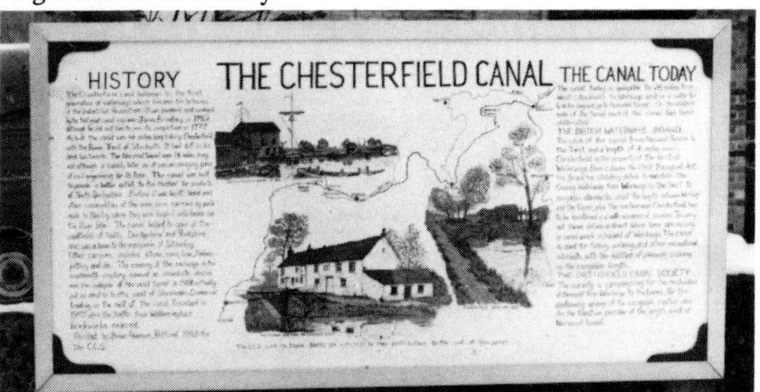

CHESTERFIELD CANAL HISTORY BOARD

CHESTERFIELD CANAL—WALK 2—KILLAMARSH—*4 miles*

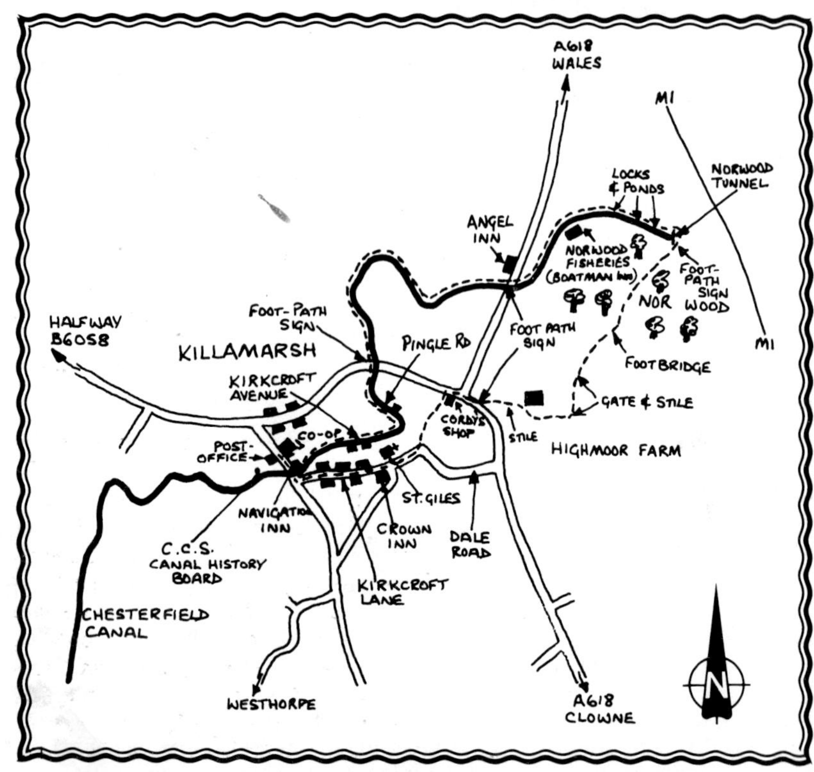

FORMER BOATMAN'S INN

CHESTERFIELD CANAL—WALK 2—
4 miles—*allow 2 hours*

ROUTE—*Killamarsh—Chesterfield Canal—Norwood—Norwood Tunnel—Nor Wood—Church Town—Killamarsh.*

MAPS—O.S. 1:50,000 Sheet No 120—Mansfield and The Dukeries —O.S. 1:25,000 Sheet No SK 48/58—Kiveton Park

CAR PARK—*Behind Co-Op store in central Killamarsh.*

ABOUT THE WALK—one of my favourites! A splendid walk following the line of the canal weaving its way through Killamarsh to Norwood. Here the canal can be seen in true splendour to Norwood Fisheries—the former Boatman Inn. From here you trace the line of the locks to the bricked up entrance of the Norwood Tunnel. To return you walk through the woodland of Nor Wood and descend the fields to Church Town and back to central Killamarsh.

WALKING INSTRUCTIONS—From the car park return to the main road—Bridge Street—with the Post Office opposite and turn left. A few yards later pass the Navigation Inn on your left. Just afterwards reach the line of the canal. To your right is a Chesterfield Canal Society history board. Turn left and follow the canal. After 200 yards the canal has been built upon but continue keeping close to its line by following Kirkcroft Avenue for a short distance, until you can regain the canal line on your right. Again you follow it for a short distance before more houses obscure its line. Here follow Pingle Road for about 40 yards before turning right to regain the canal line.From now onwards you follow the canal without interruption. Cross the B6058 road and the canal soon becomes water filled as you pass a small industrial estate on your left. ½ mile later cross the A618 road with the Angel Inn on your left. The canal is now in good order as you follow the signed track—Norwood Fisheries.

Beyond the fisheries keep beside the canal on your right as you ascend past the series of locks and ponds. In ¼ mile reach the bricked up entrance to Norwood Tunnel. Just before it turn left and ascend round above it to path and footpath sign into Nor Wood. Follow the distinct path through the wood for ½ mile, ignoring all side trails. Descend to a footbridge and stile on the woods perimeter. Bear right and ascend the field keeping the field boundary on your right. Pass through two stiles by gates before following the track round to your right to Highmoor Farm. Follow the track round to the lefthand side of it and where the farm track turns left, keep ahead past the implement sheds to a stile. Descend the field beyond to another stile and path sign beside the A618 road. Turn right and cross the road to Cordy's shop. Just past it turn left and follow the descending path to Dale Road. Ascend the road to your right to pass the parish church dedicated to St. Giles and the Crown Inn on your left. Continue ahead along Kirkcroft Lane to join Bridge Street ¼ mile later.Turn right and pass the canal and Navigation Inn you walked along at the beginning. Opposite the Post Office turn right for the car park.

NORWOOD TUNNEL ENTRANCE—CHESTERFIELD SIDE

CHESTERFIELD CANAL— WALK 3—*THORPE SALVIN—3 miles*

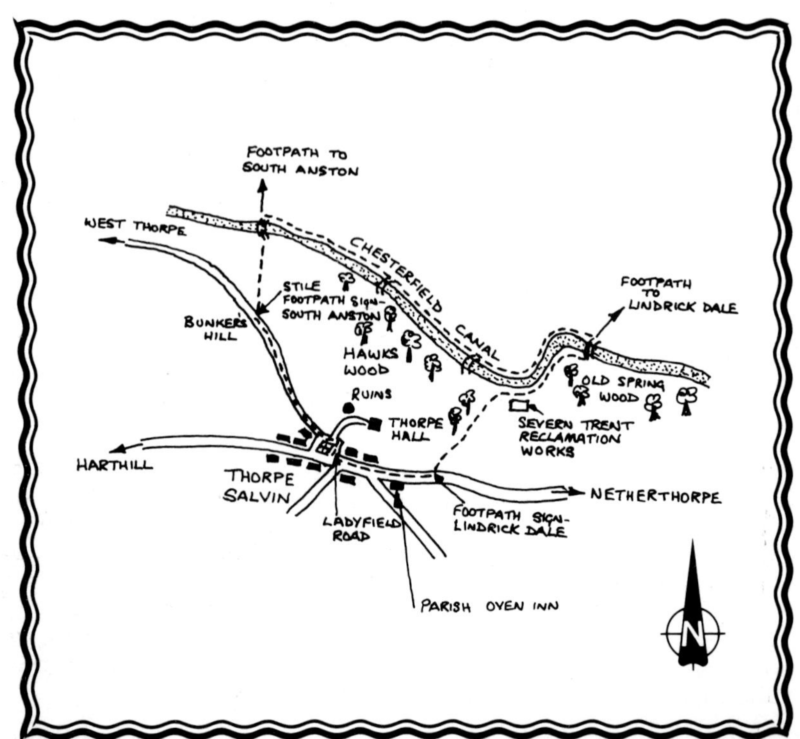

FOOTBRIDGE AND CHESTERFIELD CANAL

CHESTERFIELD CANAL—WALK 3—
allow 1½ hours

ROUTE—*Thorpe Salvin—Chesterfield Canal—Thorpe Salvin*

MAPS—*O.S. 1:50,000—Sheet No 120—Mansfield and The Dukeries*
—O.S. 1:25,000—Sheet No SK 48/58—Kiveton Park

CAR PARK—*No official one*

ABOUT THE WALK—You start at Thorpe Salvin an "unspoilt" gem of the area, with a fascinating church and old font, and the ruins of a hall nearby. After a short road walk you descend the fields to the disused Chesterfield Canal, which you follow through woodland. You return over the fields to Thorpe Salvin.

WALKING INSTRUCTIONS—Turn right in front of the churchyard into Ladyfield Road. The road curves round to your left, with the churchyard on your left and ruined hall on your right. Keep on this road for ½ mile to the top of Bunker's Hill where there is a stile and footpath sign on your right—"South Anston". Turn right and descend the edge of the field with the hedge on your right. Just after entering the trees you cross Thorpe Bridge with the canal on your right.

Turn right and walk along the towpath with the canal on your immediate right for the next 1½ miles. At the third bridge, just after passing a series of small locks on your right, cross the bridge and turn right to follow the path through the trees of Old Spring Wood. At first you are not far from the canal but just over ¼ mile and guided by yellow arrows you move away from it to gain a track in front of a Severn Trent Reclamation works. Just afterwards turn left and follow the stiled path with Old Meadow Wood on your right. ¼ mile later reach the minor road beside the footpath sign—Lindrick Dale. Turn right passing the playing fields on your right before descending past the houses to Thorpe Salvin church.

THORPE SALVIN—The ruined hall was built by the Sanfords in the 16th century. Later it was owned by the Osbourne family and Sir Thomas Osbourne, who became the Duke of Leeds, lived here until 1697 before moving to a new mansion at Kiveton Park. Since then the hall has never been lived in and is now an impressive ruin. The church is particularly interesting with considerable Norman workmanship and an exceptionally fine Norman font.

CHESTERFIELD CANAL– WALK 4–*WORKSOP–4 miles*

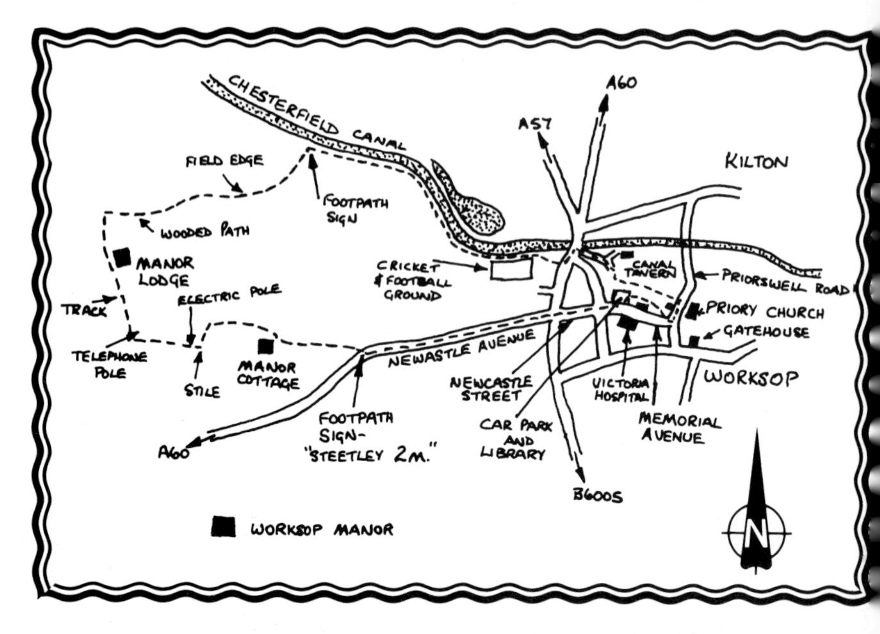

CHESTERFIELD CANAL IN WORKSOP

CHESTERFIELD CANAL—WALK 4—
4 miles—*allow 2 hours*

ROUTE— *Worksop—Chesterfield Canal—Manor Lodge—Worksop.*

MAPS— *O.S. 1:50,000 Sheet No 120—Mansfield and The Dukeries—O.S. 1:25,000 Sheet No sk 47/57—Worksop (South) & Staveley*

CAR PARK— *off Central Avenue, beside Chesterfield Canal*

ABOUT THE WALK— Worksop, known as the gateway to the Dukeries, is full of interesting and historical features, including Worksop Priory. Surprisingly you hardly see the busy shopping area before walking along the banks of the peaceful canal. You loop round the area to see the Elizabethan Manor Lodge, associated with Worksop Manor, which played a major part in both local and national history with the 'imprisonment' of the captive Mary, Queen of Scots, here in 1570. A walk across the fields returns you to Worksop.

WALKING INSTRUCTIONS— At the far end of the car park on your right gain access to the canal and turn left. Follow the towpath along the lefthand side of the canal for the next mile. At the wooden footpath sign turn left past a bridge and cross the new bypass. The path is defined and keeps to the righthand edge of the field. After ½ mile you cross a track and enter a wooded section with the remains of a canal on your right and the river Ryton on your left. Less than ¼ mile later you reach a track and turn left and walk past Manor Lodge. After the Lodge Farm on your right you pass a small wood on your left before passing fields. Continue ahead for about 150 yards and just at a telephone pole turn left and cross the field, passing an electric pole at the other side. The path line here is faint but at the hedge is a stile. Over this turn left to the field corner and gap. Through this turn right along the field edge to Manor Cottage. Turn right then left past the the buildings and continue on a defined path along the righthand perimeter of the field. Upon reaching the housing estate, bear left along the road which swings to your right to the A60 road and footpath sign—Steetley 2 miles. Turn left along Newcastle Avenue (A57) road. At the traffic lights in the centre of Worksop turn left past the shops to the car park. Just ahead is the canal bridge and Victoria Square. The Canal Tavern is not far away and is reached via Church Walk on your right to Canal Road.

MANOR LODGE— Elizabethan building designed by Robert Smythson in the late 16th century. He also designed the Manor which was later destroyed by fire.

CHESTERFIELD CANAL— WALK 5—*WORKSOP—6 miles*

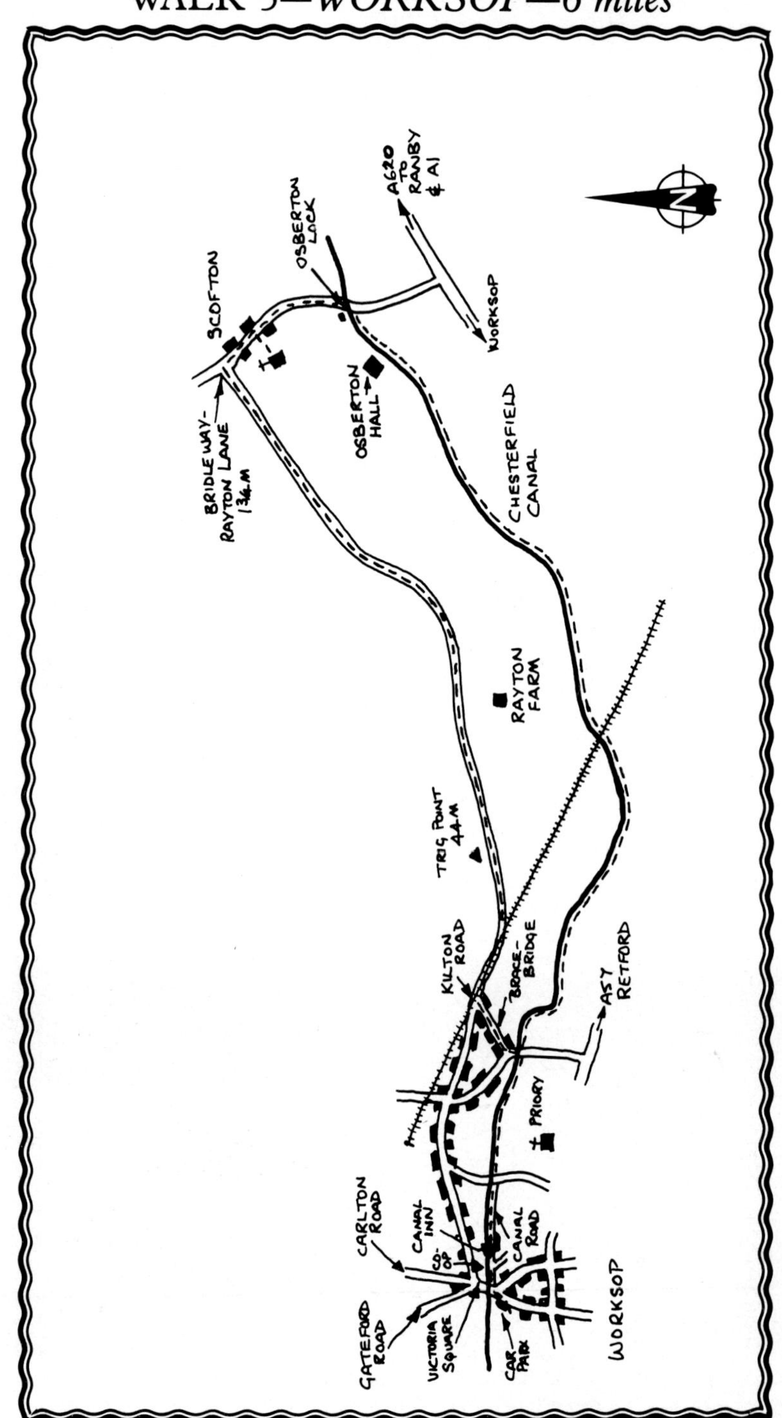

CHESTERFIELD CANAL—WALK 5—
6 miles—*allow 3 hours*

ROUTE— *Worksop—Chesterfield Canal—Osberton Lock—Scofton—Rayton Lane—Worksop.*

MAPS— *1:50,000 Sheet No 120—Mansfield and The Dukeries —1:25,000 Sheet No SK 47/57—Worksop (South) & Stavely—1:25,000 Sheet No SK 67/77—Clumber Park and East Markham —1:25,000 Sheet No SK 68/78—Retford*

CAR PARK— *off Central Avenue, beside Chesterfield Canal, in the centre of Worksop.*

ABOUT THE WALK— From the centre of Worksop you follow the start of the navigable section of the canal, for three miles to Osberton Lock. The canal section embraces the canal through industry and housing to fields and woodland sections. To return you walk through the village of Scofton on the Osberton estate before following a track then road with views of the canal, back to Kilton Lock. Here you retrace your steps back to central Worksop.

WALK INSTRUCTIONS— Walk to Central Avenue and turn left to Bridge Place where turn left. Shortly afterwards and before the canal bridge before Victoria Square and the Co-Op store, turn right into Church Walk. Turn left almost immediately into Canal Road and here you are beside the canal with the Canal Tavern on your right. Walk along the road and, at the first canal bridge, leave the road and follow the tow path. The next road bridge at Bracebridge Lock (B6041) is where you will rejoin your starting out path. Keep beside the canal for the next 3 miles to Osberton Lock.

Here leave the canal and follow the road into Scofton village. After ¼ mile pass the footpath sign to the church. 40 yards later turn left, as bridlepath signed—Rayton Lane 1¾ miles. At first you follow a fenced track, through the estate and beside woodland before reaching the tarmaced surface of Rayton Lane. Later you pass the trig point—44 metres—on your right, beside a narrow strip of woodland. Upon reaching the houses and road junction at Kilton, turn left onto Kilton Road and pass under the railway line and follow the road round to your right. Turn left along Bracebridge road and follow this to the B6041 raod (High Hoe Road). Turn left then right to rejoin the canal and retrace your steps back into Worksop.

OSBERTON HALL— the home of the Foljambe family. The present building dates from 1800 and was designed by William Wilkins. Dressage and sheep-dog trails are held on the estate. Scofton is the only village on the estate and the church which contains monuments to the Foljambe family, was built in 1833, in Norman style.

CHESTERFIELD CANAL— WALK 6—*RANBY—5 miles*

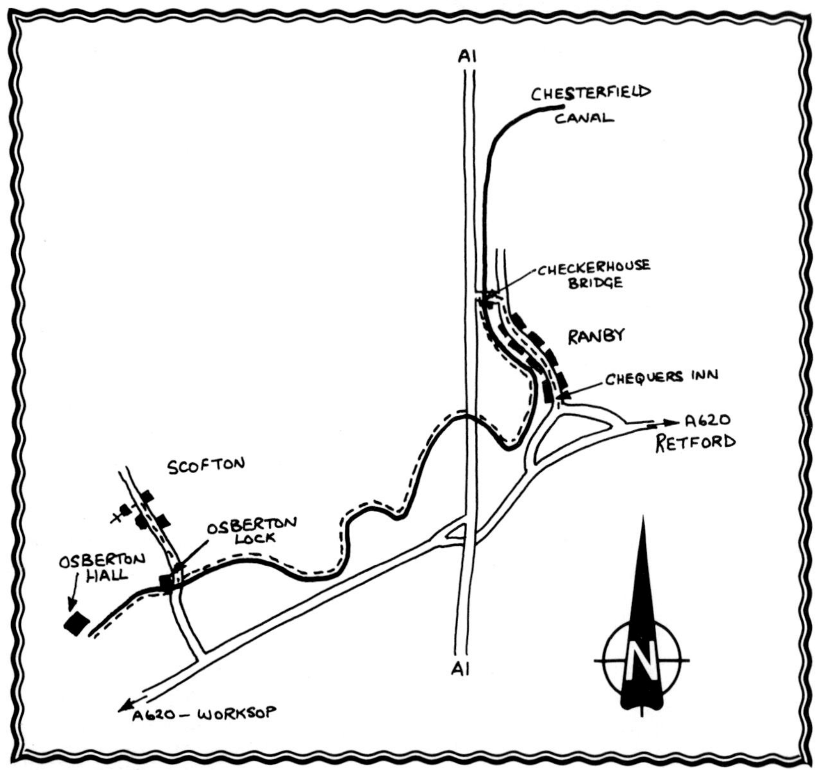

CHECKERHOUSE BRIDGE, RANBY

CHESTERFIELD CANAL—WALK 6—
5 miles—*allow 2½ hours*

ROUTE—*Ranby—Chesterfield Canal—Osberton Lock—Scofton—Chesterfield Canal—Ranby.*

MAPS—*1:50,000 Sheet No 120—Mansfield and The Dukeries —1:25,000 Sheet No 68/78—Retford*

CAR PARK—*no official one in Ranby.*

ABOUT THE WALK—a delightful walk illustrating how the early canal builders hugged the contours of the landscape. You follow the canal to Osberton Lock. Here you can enter the Osberton estate and visit Scofton church. You return the same way and the only inn is the Chequers Inn in Ranby—on the opposite side of the canal!

WALKING INSTRUCTIONS—Walk through the village of Ranby to Chequer House Bridge. Cross it and turn left past the house to the tow path. Follow the canal for the next 2½ miles, westwards as it snakes its way across the landscape. First pass the Chequers Inn on your left on the otherside of the canal. Next pass under the A1 and continue to Osberton Lock. Here leave the canal and turn right on the road to Scofton village, ¼ mile away. To visit the church turn left in the village, as footpath signed. Retrace your steps back to Osberton Lock and Ranby. A short distance along the canal on your right at Osberton Lock will take you past Osberton Hall—see Walk No 5.

OSBERTON LOCK

CHESTERFIELD CANAL— WALK 7—*RETFORD*—*5½ miles*

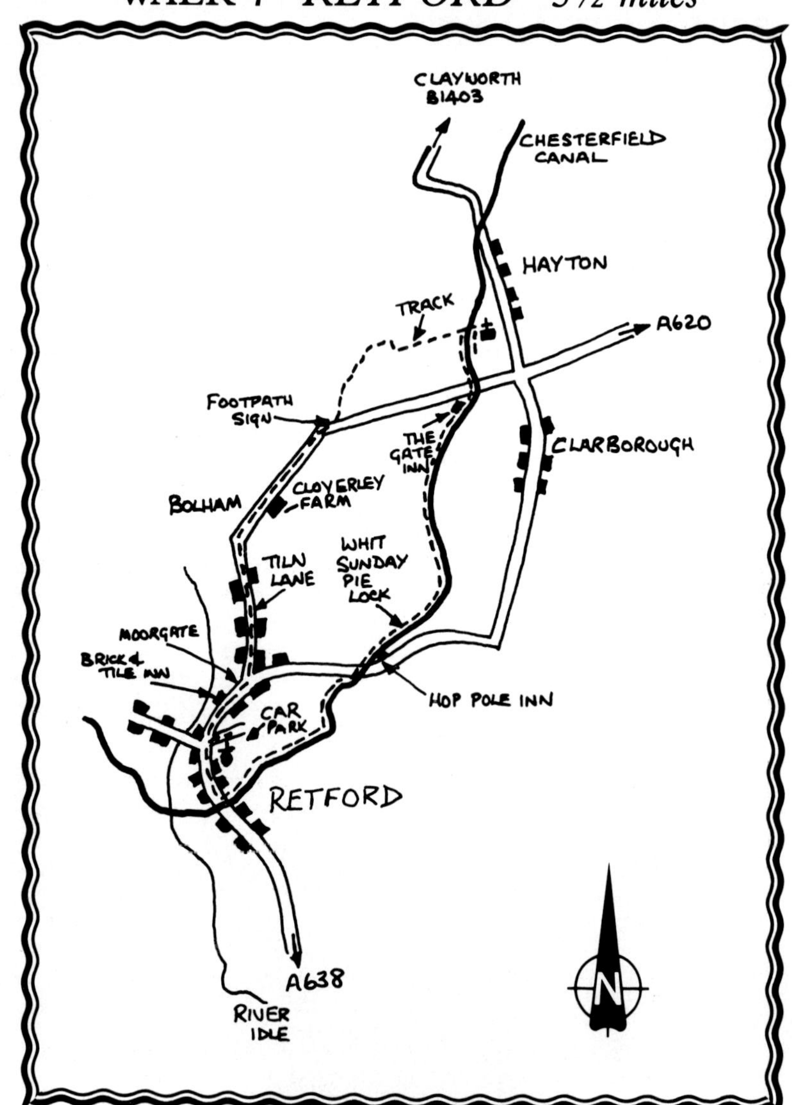

BRICK & TILE INN, RETFORD

CHESTERFIELD CANAL—WALK 7—
5½ miles—*allow 3 hours*

ROUTE—*Retford—Chesterfield Canal—Hayton—Bolham—Retford.*

MAPS—*1:50,000 Sheet No 120—Mansfield and The Dukeries —1:25,000 Sheet No 68/78—Retford*

CAR PARK—*Chapelgate*

ABOUT THE WALK—Leaving the confines of Retford and its interesting buildings—worth exploring later—you follow the canal northwards past Whit Sunday Pie Lock to Hayton. Opposite the church you leave the canal to cross fields and follow a road back to Retford. There is some really enjoyable walking here and from Hayton you can extend the walk along the canal to Clayworth and Wiseton. On your return you can cross Chain Bridge Road to visit the Wetlands Waterfowl Reserve, off Lound Low Road, in Sutton-cum-Lound. A look at the map will indicate the possibilities and a day exploring this area of the canal is extremely enjoyable.

WALKING INSTRUCTIONS—Turn left out of the car park into Chapelgate; opposite is St.Swithin's church. Turn left almost immediately into Churchgate and walk past the shops into the Market Square. Continue ahead into Carolgate, passing Boots, Preedy's,the Anchor Inn, and the Packet Inn. Turn left at the bridge and descend to the tow path. To your right is the Retford Basin. Keep the canal on your right for the next 2½ miles. You pass under two bridges before reaching Hop Pole Bridge—A620 with the Hop Pole Inn on your right. ¼ mile later you reach the Whit Sunday Pie lock. The next mile is quiet, peaceful walking to the Gate Inn. Pass under another bridge and ¼ mile later with Hayton church on your right, leave the canal at the bridge, and follow the fenced track to your left.

Keep on the track which after ¼ mile bears right. Just afterwards turn left onto a hedged track and follow it to a large field. The pathline from here is faint and basically goes diagonally left across the fields. It is simpler to keep to the field edge for the next ½ mile to the minor road from Clarborough. The exit to the road is in the righthand corner of the field, where there is a footbridge and path sign. Bear right and follow the lane past Cloverley Farm to the road junction. Turn left towards Retford on Tiln Lane. A little over ½ mile later reach the A620 road. Turn right along it—Moorgate—passing the Brick and Tile Inn. At the main road turn left along Arlington Way and opposite the New Sun Inn, right into Chapelgate.

RETFORD—The town, one of the oldest boroughs in England, is split in half by the River Idle and known as East and West Retford. The Market Square has numerous Georgian buildings, with the White Hart Inn nearby, a former coaching inn. In front of the Town Hall are the remains of a boundary cross, known as the Broad Stone. Originally it stood several hundred yards away and during the plague this was as near as the people came. Money would be left in vinegar water for payment for food—as was done at Eyam in Derbyshire. A copy of a 'recipe against the plague', written into the East Retford church (St.Swithins) register can be obtained from the church, and dates from the early 18th century. St Swithin's church is worth visiting and like much of Retford in 1528 was burnt down. The present building was largely rebuilt in 1658 and contains a 15th century font, a turret clock dated 1673 and some really fine stained glass windows. Outside is Cannon Square with a cannon from the Battle of Sebastopol in 1858.

CHESTERFIELD CANAL— WALK 8—*MISTERTON—3½ miles*

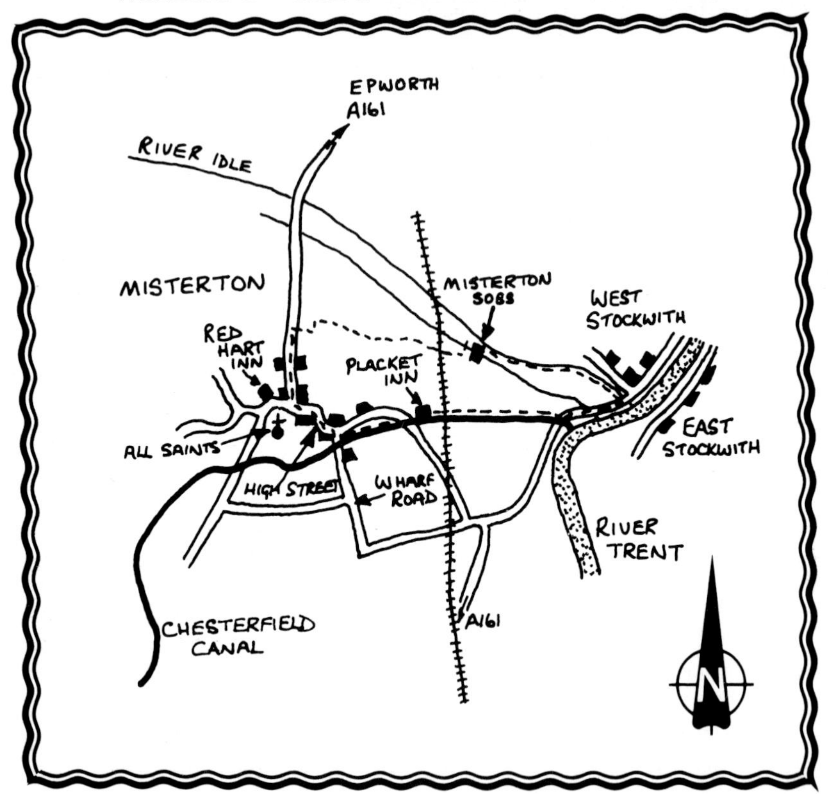

WEST STOCKWITH BASIN

CHESTERFIELD CANAL—WALK 8—
3½ miles—*allow 1½ hours*

ROUTE—*Misterton—Misterton Soss—River Idle—West Stockwith—Chesterfield Canal—Misterton.*

MAPS—*1:50,000 Sheet No 112—Scunthorpe —1:25,000 Sheet No SK 69/79 —Bawtry*

CAR PARK—*no official one in Misterton.*

ABOUT THE WALK—a short walk to see where the canal joins the River Trent—almost at the Nottinghamshire/South Yorkshire/Lincolnshire boundary. The area is totally flat and a great place to watch sunrise and sunset! You return along the canal to Misterton.

WALKING INSTRUCTIONS—Starting from All Saints church in Misterton, follow the A161 road towards Haxey for 100 yards, passing Church Street and the Red Hart Inn on your left. A little past the Old Vicarage and The Rookery, turn right at the footpath sign—Misterton Soss 1 mile. After 20 yards and in the first field turn left to a stile. Over this turn right with the hedge on your right, to a 3 way footpath sign—Misterton Soss ¾ mile, West Stockwith 1¾ miles. Continue across the field to another path sign, where you keep the field boundary on your right. ¼ mile later gain the railway line and cross it, continuing on a good path towards the twin chimneys of Misterton Soss—an old pumping station. At the road turn left over the bridge and right onto the banks of River Idle. Follow the top of the bank for ¾ mile to West Stockwith.

Reaching the road—Canal Lane—turn right past the houses and over the Mother Drain, with the River Trent on your left. Leave the road at West Stockwith basin and the Chesterfield Canal; on your right is the Crown Inn. Follow the tow path with the canal on your left. In a little over ½ mile pass under the railway and emerge at the Packet Inn. Continue beside the canal past Misterton lock under another bridge to the next one, crossed by Wharf Road. Ascend to the road and turn right along it into Misterton. At the main road—A161—continue ahead along the High Street to return you to All Saints church.

MISTERTON—All Saints church was restored in 1848 and contains many memorials to rope makers and shipwrights. The Packet Inn recalls the time when sail boats passed along the canal to Retford.

WEST STOCKWITH—The basin is quite large to accommodate the barges and canal boats for loading and unloading. The scene is still a busy one today with numerous boats travelling on the canal or River Trent reached via the West Stockwith Lock. The village was once very busy with goods being shipped down the River Idle from Bawtry. There was a ferry across the River Trent to East Stockwith which ran for 400 years until 1952; today it is 15 miles by road. St. Mary's church was built in 1722, funded by a wealthy ship-owner, William Huntington.

PACKET INN

BEESTON MARINA

CHESTERFIELD CANAL—WALK 9—
26 miles

ROUTE—*Worksop to West Stockwith via Chesterfield Canal.*

MAPS—*1:50,000 Sheet No 120—Mansfield and The Dukeries —1:50,000 Sheet No 112—Scunthorpe*

ABOUT THE WALK—The navigable section of the canal from Worksop to the River Trent at Stockwith makes an ideal walk and, with inns at regular intervals, a really long pub crawl! You can walk it either as a challenge walk from end to end in a day or do it in sections, savouring the beauty of the surrounding area. You will have to road walk round the Drakeholes Tunnel.

I suggest the following stages—

Worksop to Ranby—*5 miles*
Ranby to East Retford—*5 miles*
East Retford to Hayton—*3½ miles*
Hayton via Clayworth to Wiseton—*4½ miles*
Wiseton via Misterton to West Stockwith—*8 miles*

WHIT SUNDAY PIE LOCK

CROMFORD CANAL

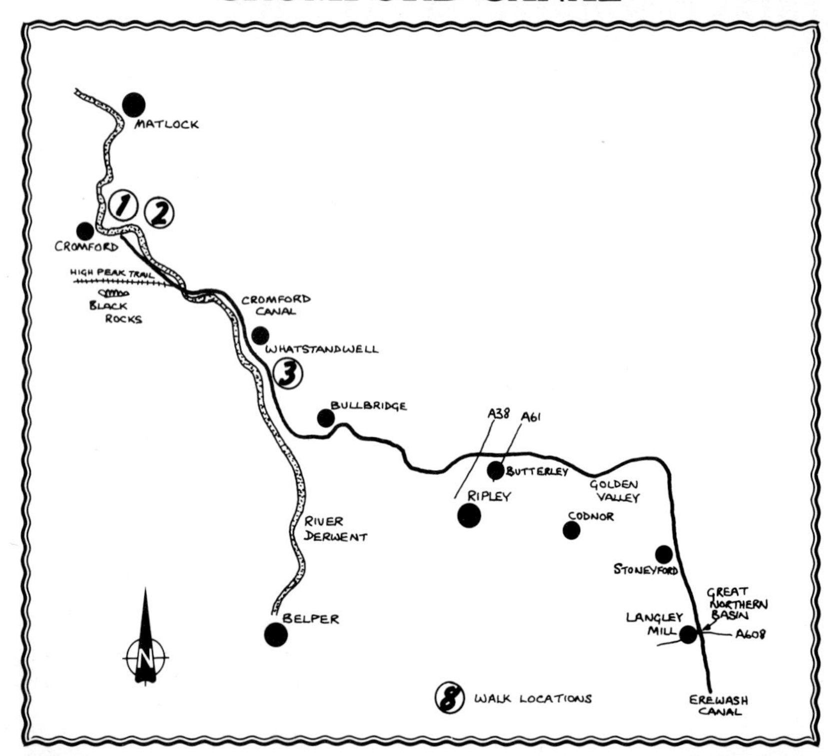

LEAWOOD PUMP HOUSE

CROMFORD CANAL

Completed in 1794; engineered by William Jessop and Benjamin Outram at a cost of £78,900.

Length—14½ miles from Cromford to the Erewash Canal at Langley Mill; passing through Stoneyford, Codnor Park, Butterley, Ambergate (Bullbridge) and Whatstandwell. There were 14 locks from Langley Mill to Codnor from where it was level to Cromford. En route were four tunnels—Gregory Tunnel is 76 yards long—but the biggest was Butterley at 3,063 yards long. There was no tow path and the tunnel was only 7 feet wide. Boats entered the eastern end between 5 and 6 a.m. and 1 and 2 p.m. and the western end between 9 and 10 a.m. and 5 and 6 p.m. Boats were allowed three hours to get through.

Sir Richard Arkwright was a key figure in its development but died before it was complete. For a while it proved a useful link in the canal system but the coming of the railway in the 1870's forced it into decline. The Butterley tunnel finally collapsed in 1900 and the canal was closed to through traffic. From 1944 no section of the canal was used. Much now has been filled in but the 5 mile section from Cromford Wharf to Ambergate is being preserved. The Derbyshire County Council took it over in 1974 and the Cromford Canal Society have undertaken a considerable amount of work at Cromford Wharf and Leawood Pumphouse. The latter is open on specific days and during the summer horse-drawn canal trips operate from Cromford Wharf.

CROMFORD WHARF—warehouse, counting house, cottages and smithy date from the early days of the canal. Opposite is Arkwright's cotton mill which is open during the summer and run by the Arkwright Society.

HIGH PEAK JUNCTION—The Peak District terrain was impracticable for the construction of a canal. A tramway linked the Cromford Canal with the Peak Forest Canal at Whaley Bridge, 33 miles away. Here the goods were transferred to wagons and were hauled up the first incline to begin the three day journey to Whaley Bridge. The tramway was opened in 1831.

LEAWOOD PUMP HOUSE—Inside is a large beam engine built by Graham and Co., of Elsecar, Yorkshire and was installed in 1849. The canal was suffering from a lack of water and the engine lifted 31 tons of water a minute from the river Derwent below.

DERWENT HOTEL, Whatstandwell—Takes its name from the river but was originally the Bull's Head. Here in coaching days the coaches stopped for refreshment before ascending the hill to Crich. The name Whatstandwell is from Walter Stonewell who built a bridge here in the 14th century. Last century it was known as Hot-Stanwell and Will't stand well?

BULLBRIDGE—The remains of the aquaduct are all that is left of a 200 yard long, 50 foot high aquaduct over the river Amber, railway and A610 built in 1793 by William Jessop. Also to be seen is a swing horse-bridge.

End to End Canal walk—From Cromford Wharf to the canal's end at Bullbridge is 5 miles and makes a very pleasant walk in its own right, either as a one way walk or as a ten mile return walk. The wildlife on the canal area is prolific and I have seen more moorhens, owls, water voles and grey squirrels here than anywhere. On one occasion I saw a 3 foot long adder, the biggest snake I have seen in Britain.

CROMFORD CANAL—
WALK 1 & 2—*CROMFORD—3 & 7 miles*

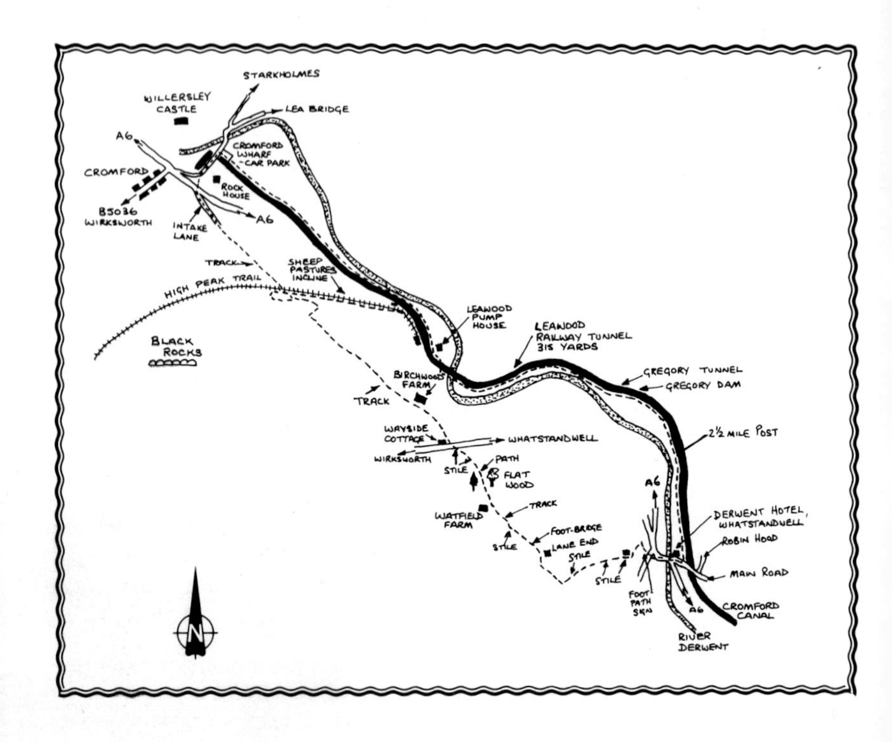

Descend the next field, passing Lane End on your right to a stile close to two greenhouses. The path line is now well defined with prominent stile signs. Cross the track to Watergate Farm to a stile and footbridge shortly after. You now begin to ascend with the stonewall on your right. Beyond reach a stile and 30 yards later the track to Watfield Farm. Turn left along this past two cottages on your right. Upon approaching the farm turn right beside it up a walled track to a stile. Continue ahead to another and follow the path beside the wall along the edge of woodland.At the next stile you enter the woodland and descend to the Wirksworth Road at Longway Bank. Cross to the tarmaced lane beside Wayside Cottage to Birchwood Farm. You now keep on this for the next mile. The lane soon becomes a track and after a mile you reach woodland beside a footpath sign—Alderwasley/Cromford. Turn right along the track which soon turns left as you descend to the tunnel beneath the High Peak Trail. Here the shorter route joins. Pass under the trail and follow the track—Intake Lane—as you descend to the outskirts of Cromford; the track now becoming a tarmaced road. Continue to the A6 road. Cross to your right to the bollard and path past Rock House on your right. Gain the road in front of Cromford Mill and turn right to Cromford Wharf.

CROMFORD CANAL—
WALKS 1 and 2—
3 and 7 miles—*allow 2 and 4 hours.*

ROUTE—*Cromford Wharf—Canal—High Peak Junction—Whatstandwell—Longway Bank—Sheep Pastures Incline—Cromford Wharf.*

MAPS—*O.S. 1:50,000 Sheet No 119—Buxton, Matlock and Dove Dale—O.S. 1:25,000—Outdoor Leisure Map—The White Peak—East sheet. —O.S 1:25,000 Sheet No SK 25/35—Matlock (South)*

CAR PARK—*Cromford Wharf.*

ABOUT THE WALKS—Cromford is an exceptional area for the industrial archaeologist—the Arkwright buildings and mills, the canal, and the High Peak Railway. The history of each is absorbing. This walk takes you to all three, and one can readily see much on location. The walk is two-tiered for you can do a short walk of three miles by ascending part of the Sheep Pastures Incline and see all three features. The longer walk of seven miles takes you along some of the most picturesque parts of the canal to an inn before walking back on the opposite side of the valley. Either walk will create a memorable outing.

WALKING INSTRUCTIONS—Walk along the lefthand bank of the canal, away from the wharf. After just over a mile you reach the High Peak Junction. Those taking the shorter route should cross the canal and ascend half the incline to a footpath sign on your left. Leave the trail here and walk under the trail, the longer route joins the route here. Those on the longer route should keep to the lefthand side of the canal and pass Leawood Pump House on your left. Just afterwards cross the footbridge and walk beside the canal, now on your left. This section of the walk is particularly attractive as the canal weaves its way through woodland and Gregory's Tunnel, past Gregory's Dam to Whatstandwell, 2 miles away. Upon reaching the road—Main Road—turn right to the A6 road and Derwent Hotel.

Cross the A6 road bridge over the river Derwent and where the road turns sharp right, continue ahead on a path to the minor road to Alderwasley. Cross over to the stile and footpath sign. Ascend the path beside the wall for about 100 yards before turning left on a path to the drive to Hilltop Farm. Cross, as footpath signposted and walk along the path with the drive on your right. Ascend the stile by the house and keep the field boundary on your left as you gently ascend. Ascend two stiles and after the next field—your third from the house—turn right and descend beside the hawthorn and holly trees to a stile in them.

HORSE DRAWN BOAT ON CROMFORD CANAL

CROMFORD CANAL–
WALK 3–*WHATSTANDWELL–7 miles*

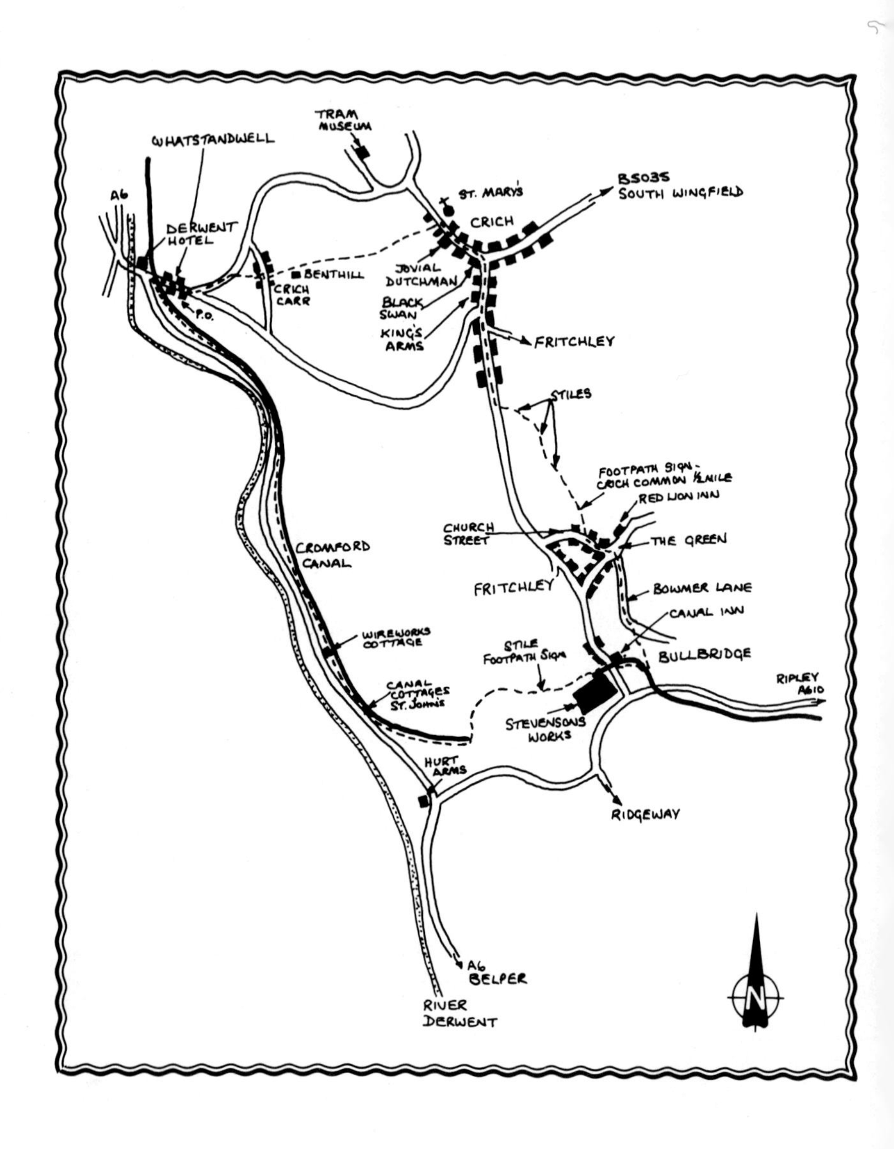

immediately and descend more steps to Glen Road. Where this turns right, keep ahead and descend the narrow lane into Hinderstich Lane, which descend to the Main Road in Whatstandwell. Turn right past the Post Office on your left back to the canal and starting point.

CROMFORD CANAL—WALK 3—
7 miles—*allow 3½ hours*

ROUTE— *Whatstandwell—Cromford Canal—Bullbridge—Fritchley—Crich Common—Crich—Crich Carr—Whatstandwell.*

MAPS— *O.S. 1:50,000 Sheet No 119—Buxton, Matlock and Dove Dale—O.S. 1:25,000 Outdoor Leisure Map—The White Peak—East sheet—0.S. 1:25,000 Sheet No SK 25/35—Matlock (South)*

CAR PARK— *no official one.*

ABOUT THE WALK— This walk follows the canal from where the previous walk left it at Whatstandwell. You follow it to its end near Bullbridge and after walking around a works perimeter pick up a final fragment beside the Canal Inn at Bulbridge. This particular fragment is most interesting. You can either retrace your steps or as detailed ascend the fields and roads to Crich, offering views of the Amber Valley and the six sailed windmill at Nether Heage. Crich is full of interesting buildings and the walk can be extended by ½ mile to visit the Tramway Museum. You descend the fields back to Whatstandwell.

WALKING INSTRUCTIONS— Turn right at the canal, just up the road from the Derwent Hotel, beside the A6. Follow the tow path on the righthand side of the canal for just over 2 miles to its end. As footpath signposted at the end, turn left and walk around the perimeter fence of the works. Keep close to the fence and begin ascending gently. In the final stages you walk up a track to a path sign. Here turn right through a stile and follow the path to a long flight of steps. Descend these to a T junction of paths, turn left and follow the path beside another fence, around Stevensons factory. At the end gain the road at Bullbridge. Opposite is the final fragment of the canal and just up the road is the Canal Inn. Cross the road and follow the path beside the canal to the start of the aquaduct. This has now been demolished. Follow the path down to the railway line. Don't cross it but turn left along the path beneath the start of the aquaduct. Pass through the stile and turn right, along the tarred track and follow it as it curves left under a tramway bridge, past the houses—Coppers and Stride n' arf. Just afterwards at the bend continue ahead and ascend the steps. At the top bear right along the path which will eventually bring you to Bowmer Lane, beside Amberley House. Turn left and walk along the road to Fritchley.

Cross The Green—the Red Lion Inn is on your right—and ascend Church Street. Opposite House No 8 turn right onto a small No Through Road and follow it round to Greenfields. There is a small chapel on the left at the start—now a private house. At the end of the road beside Greenfields, pass through the stile, following the signed path— Crich Common ½ mile. The path is defined and well stiled as you cross the fields beside gritstone walls. At the end turn left along a track to the road and turn right. Follow the road into Crich, passing the King's Arms on your left, The Dimple on your right and three-storied stockinger's house on your left. Continue ahead through the village past the Post Office and Black Swan Inn to the Cross restored in 1871. Again continue ahead passing the Jovial Dutchman Inn to St. Mary's church. Just before it leave the road at house No 9 and follow the well stiled path across the fields, heading almost due west. After the third field you begin descending to the right of Benthill. After ½ mile from Crich, cross Benthill track and descend the stone steps to the road at Crich Carr, beside Hilltop Cottages. Bear right then left

NOTTINGHAM, BEESTON, EREWASH, NUTBROOK, AND DERBY CANALS

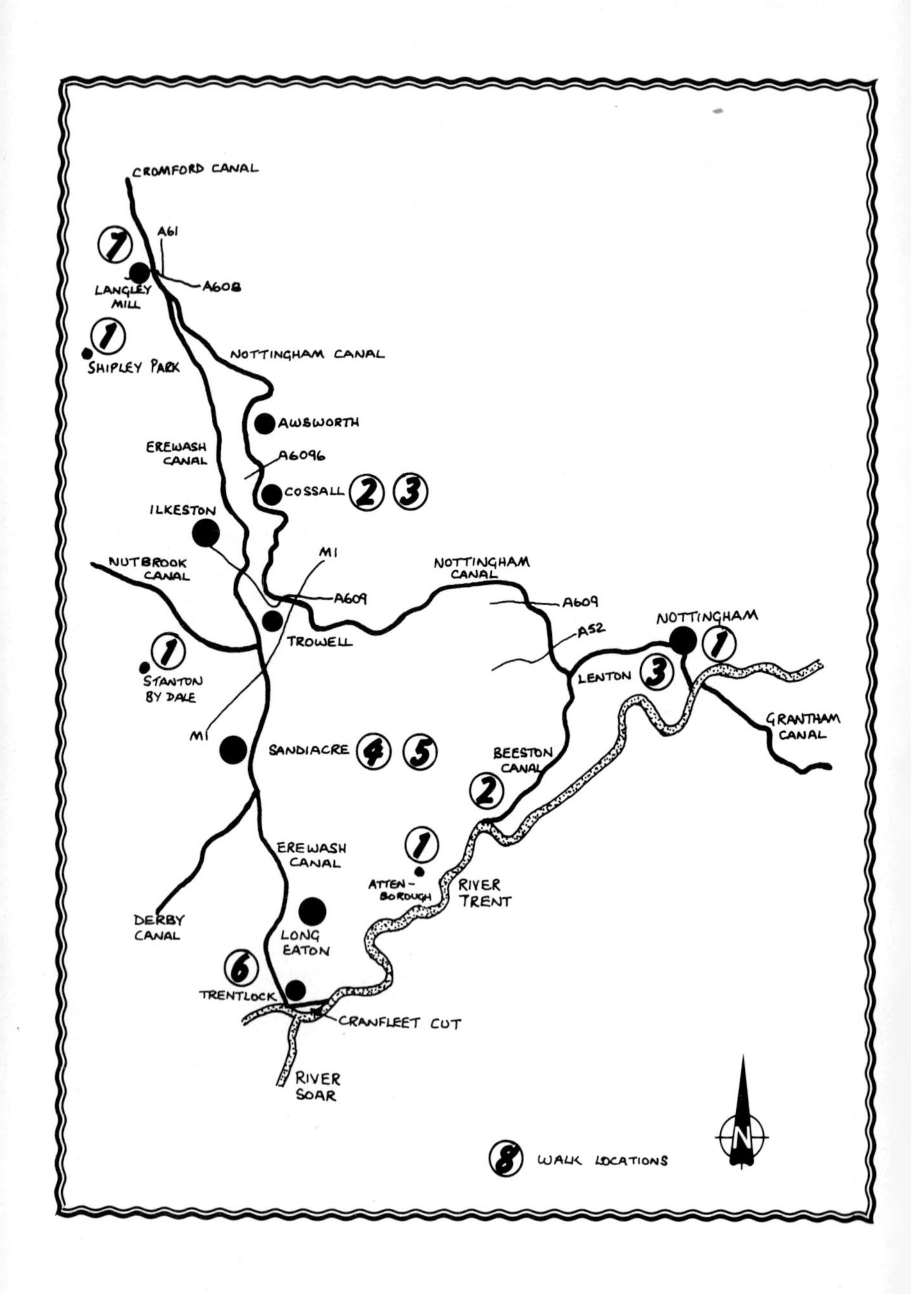

EREWASH CANAL

Authorised in 1777. Capital of £23,000 was raised by £100 shares. John Varley, who had been involved with the Chesterfield Canal, was appointed the engineer at a salary of £220 per annum. Pinkerton Brothers were the joint contractors. The canal was opened in July 1779 and had taken only 20 months to dig at a cost of £21,000. The canal—11¾ miles long—ran from Trentlock to Langley Mill, closely following the river Erewash. In its length were 14 locks rising 109 feet from Trentlock to Langley Mill. The locks were wide gauge to take the Upper Trent Wide Boats which were 70 feet long by 14 feet wide.

The relatively cheap cost of the canal plus the abundance of trade from the surrounding area, made the canal one of the most prosperous in Britain. At its height a £100 share was worth £1,300 and in 1826 a dividend of 74% was paid.

The decline was partly due to the coming of the railway, being both cheaper and quicker than canals, but also because of the high tolls charged by the Erewash Canal Company. In an effort to revitalise it this century, the Grand Union Canal Company bought it in 1932, with others, but it was too late, and it was passed to the British Waterways Board upon Nationalisation. By the middle of this century it was little used and in 1962 the section from Gallows Inn in Ilkeston to Langley Mill was classed un-navigable, but was used occasionally. Six years later in 1968, the Transport Act declared the canal closed to navigation from Long Eaton to Langley Mill.

There the canal might have been left to decay and one of the great transport routes on the Midlands might have been lost. But, in 1968 a Canal Preservation Society was formed to save the canal. It has been their singlemindedness that has saved such a historic canal from abandonment. The Great Northern Basin was restored and re-opened on May 26th 1973. Almost ten years later in February 1983, the Erewash Canal was upgraded from a 'Remainder' waterway to a 'Cruiseway'.

GREAT NORTHERN INN AND BASIN

EREWASH CANAL— WALK 1—*SHIPLEY PARK—6 miles*

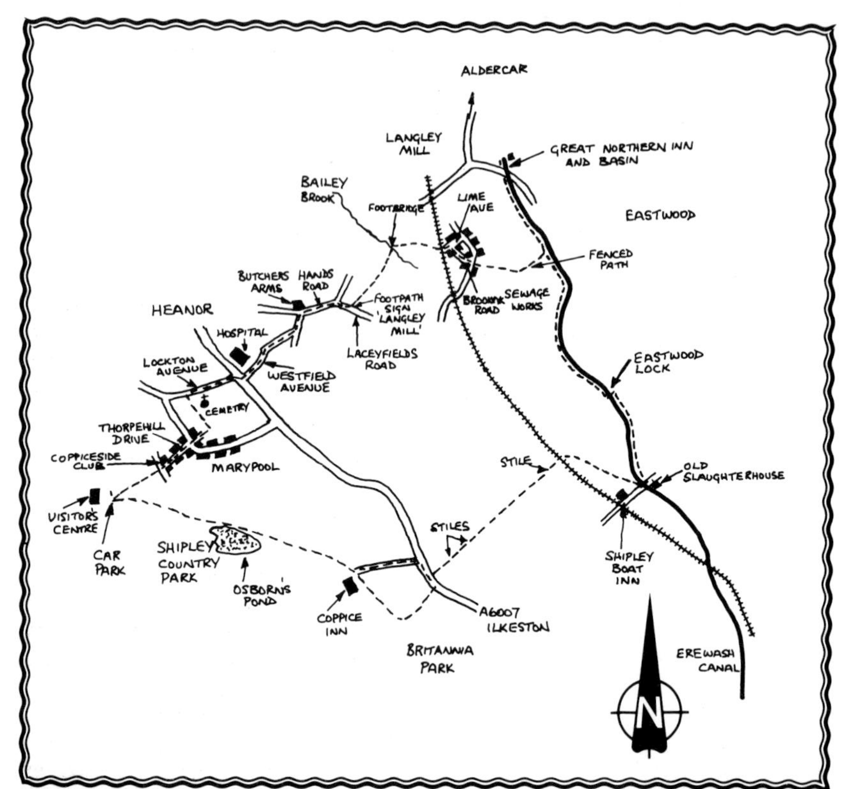

LOCK ON EREWASH CANAL

SHIPLEY COUNTRY PARK—opened in 1975 and includes the remains of Shipley Hall, its gardens and lakes. A quarter of the area was colliery waste heaps and these have been landscaped and Shipley Lake reformed. There are 17 miles of paths, a mile long trim trail, a Farmcraft Centre on Shipley Hill and a Visitors Centre.

EREWASH CANAL—WALK 1—
6 miles—with a mile extension to Great Northern Basin—*allow 3 hours*

ROUTE—*Shipley Park—Marlpool—Common Side—Heanor—Erewash Canal—Shipley Boat Inn—Shipley—Britannia Park—Shipley Park.*

MAPS—*O.S. 1:50,000 Sheet No 129—Nottingham and Loughborough—O.S. 1:25,000 Sheet No SK 44/54—Nottingham (North) and Ilkeston.*

CAR PARK—*Shipley Park—Visitor's Centre (Heanor Gate End).*

ABOUT THE WALK—The first mile involves passing through the houses of Heanor, but gives an appreciation of the setting of the Great Northern Basin, where the Cromford, Nottingham and Erewash canals met. A short one mile return walk takes you to the basin. You walk beside the canal for two miles to the Shipley Boat Inn. Here you ascend to Shipley and entrance to Britannia Park before walking through Shipley Country Park back to the visitor's Centre.

WALKING INSTRUCTIONS—Turn left at the top of the car park, first along a tarmaced road, then on a descending path to the houses and Coppice Side Club. Continue ahead along Thorpehill Drive to the main road. Cross over and first along a tarmaced drive before turning left along a path, with the cemetery over the hedge on your right. ¼ mile later reach Lockton Avenue and turn right along this to the A6007 road, with hospital opposite. Turn right then left almost immediately into Westfield Avenue. Follow this past the houses as you begin descending. At the bottom bear left to Hands Road and the Butchers Arms. Turn right along Hands Road for 100 yards before turning right into Laceyfields Road. Almost immediately on your left is a footpath sign and path. Follow this with the houses on your left to a footbridge, ¼ mile away. Cross the bridge and turn half right making for the railway tunnel. Through this enter Lime Avenue. 20 yards later turn right into Brookvik Road. At the next road junction continue ahead onto a tarmaced road, leading to the Sewage Works. Before you get there turn left along a fenced path to reach the Erewash Canal.

To reach the Great Northern Basin, turn left along the tow path for ½ a mile. The basin is impressive and on the right is the Great Northern Inn. Retrace your steps back to where you joined the canal and continue beside it (now on your left) as you follow the tow path. After a mile reach Eastwood Lock and cross over to the lefthand side and continue beside the canal (now on your right). Almost ½ mile later reach the small road bridge close to the Old Slaughter House and Shipley Boat Inn. Turn right immediately once over the bridge and follow the path beside the fence then hedge on your left. After ¼ mile bear left through a railway tunnel and keep straight ahead to a stile; ignoring the road on your left. Begin ascending gently up the field with the field boundary, after 100 yards, on your left. Keep the field boundary on your left all the time to reach the wooden stiles. After a further ¼ mile you walk beside a wood on your left.

Upon reaching the main road—A6007 at Shipley, turn left if you want to visit Britannia Park. Alternatively turn right and 100 yards later left along the road into Shipley Park. After ¼ mile turn right onto a path near the Coppice Inn. After ½ mile pass a small lake on your left before ascending back to the car park.

EREWASH CANAL—
WALK 2—*COSSALL—3 miles*

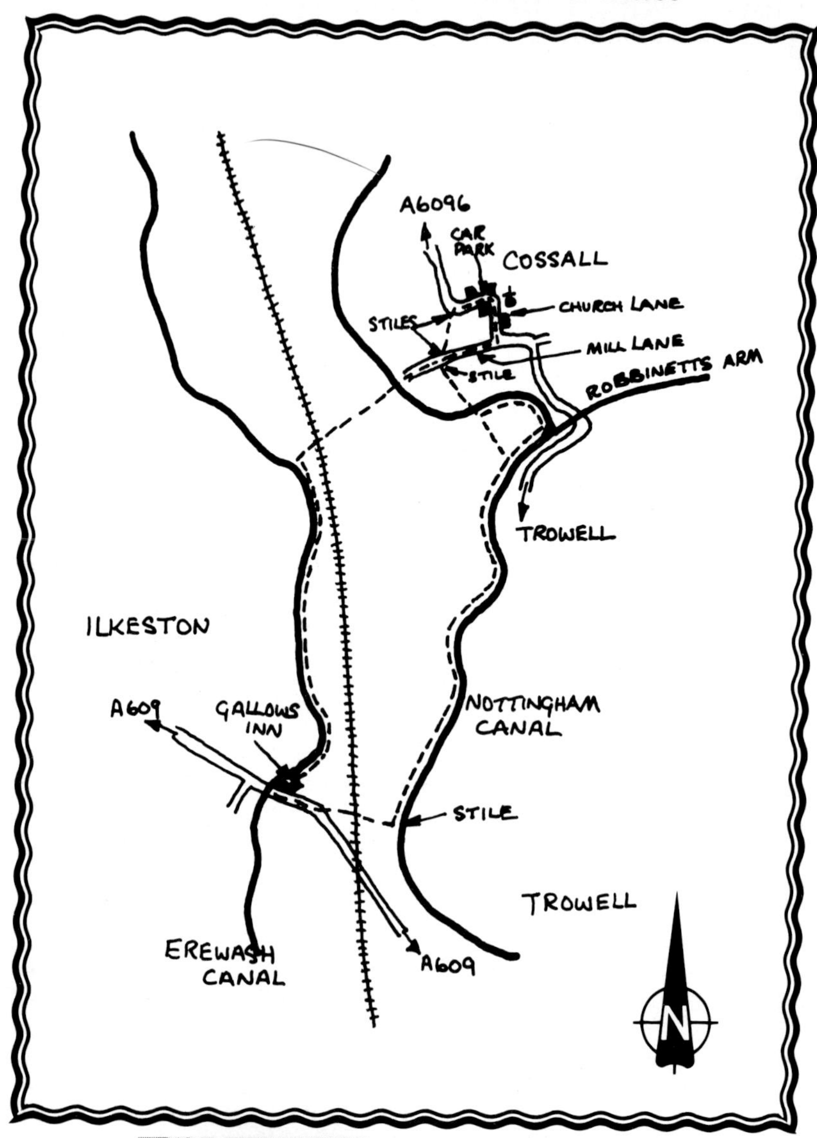

NOTTINGHAM CANAL NR. COSSALL

EREWASH CANAL—WALK 2—
3 miles—*allow 1½ hours*

ROUTE—*Cossall—Nottingham Canal—Gallows Inn—Erewash Canal —Cossall.*

MAPS—*O.S.—1:50,000—Sheet No 129—Nottingham and Loughborough—O.S.—1:25,000—Sheet No SK 44/54—Nottingham (North) and Ilkeston.*

CAR PARK—*Cossall.*

ABOUT THE WALK—A short walk linking together the Nottingham and Erewash canals; seeing a preserved one and an abandoned one. The village of Cossall is very attractive and full of history with links with D.H. Lawrence.

WALKING INSTRUCTIONS—Turn left out of the car park and follow Church Lane, past the church and down the hill. Where the road turns sharp left, turn right along Mill Lane, a signposted bridleway to the Nottingham Canal. After about 100 yards leave the track via the stile and path on your left, and cross the field to the Nottingham Canal. Cross it and turn left along the tow path and keep the canal on your left for the next 1½ miles. At first the canal does a loop contouring round the level to the junction with the Robbinetts Arm of the canal. A little over a mile later is the stile, footpath sign and path, on your right. You descend to the railway line before gaining the A6007 road, via a kissing gate beside a canal towpath sign.

Turn right and follow the road over the Erewash River (the Derbyshire/Nottinghamshire boundary) and gain the Erewash Canal moments later at Gallows Inn. Turn right along the tow path with the canal on your left. Follow the canal for a mile and just before the Ilkeston Lock, turn right along the path, first over a footbridge over the Erewash River, then across the railway line, before continuing up a track to the Nottingham Canal, ¼ mile away. Cross the canal and continue on the track, now Mill Lane that you walked along at the beginning. Instead of retracing your steps further up the lane, turn left opposite the stile and path you used earlier and ascend the field to the road in Cossall. Turn right along it past the Willoughby Almshouses to the car park.

COSSALL—The church dedicated to St. Catherine dates from the 12th century. Close to the gate is the Waterloo Memorial, 1877, recording three locals who took part in the famous battle. Church Cottage was the home of D.H. Lawrence's fiance and is featured in his novel—The Rainbow. The Willoughby Almshouses were built by George Willoughby in 1685.

CHURCH COTTAGE, COSSALL

EREWASH CANAL—
WALK 3—*COSSALL—9½ miles*

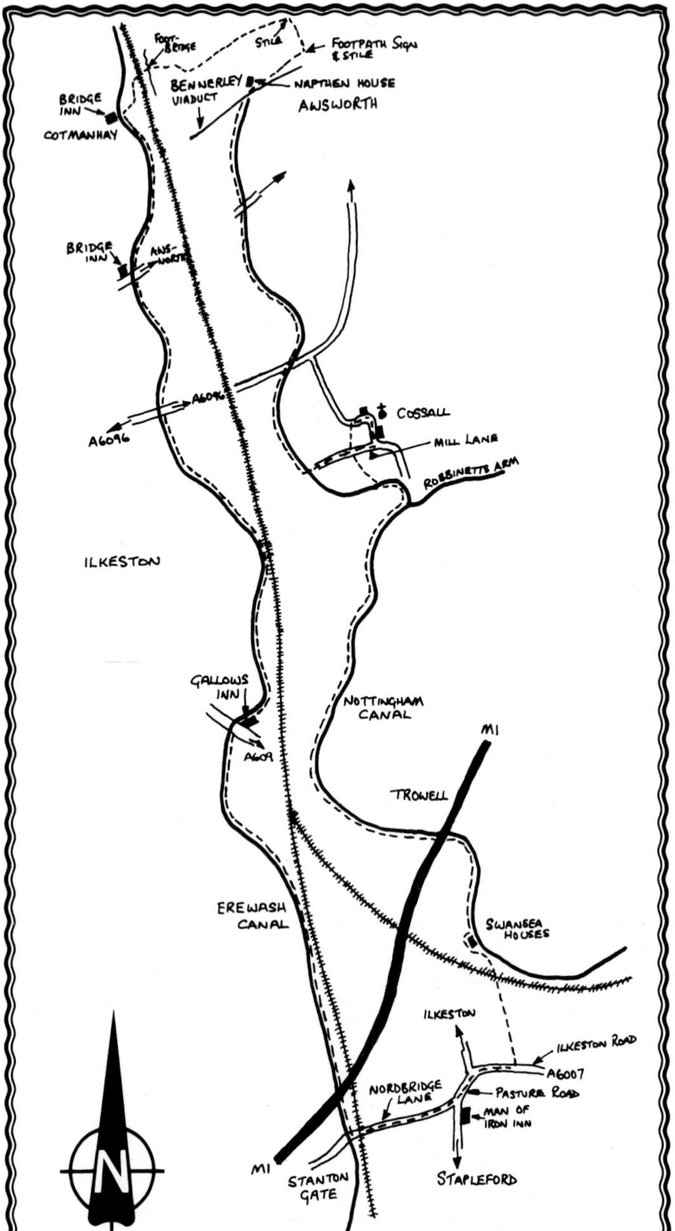

EREWASH CANAL—WALK 3—9½ miles—*allow 4 hours.*

ROUTE—*Cossall—Nottingham Canal—New Stapleford—Stanton Gate—Erewash Canal—Cotmanhay—Nottingham Canal—Cossall.*

MAPS—*1:50,000—Sheet No 129—Nottingham and Loughborough —1:25,000—Sheet No SK 44/54—Nottingham (North) and Ilkeston —1:25,000—Sheet No SK 43/53—Nottingham (South West)*

CAR PARK—*Cossall*

ABOUT THE WALK—You follow almost all that is walkable of the Nottingham Canal, using the Erewash Canal as the linking path. The contrast between a restored and navigable canal with the Nottingham Canal now derelict is an interesting comparison. A short road walk through New Stapleford links the two canals at the southern end. The northern link is mostly along paths across the fields. There are several pubs en route!

WALKING INSTRUCTIONS—Turn left out of the car park and descend Church Lane past the church. At the bottom where the road turns sharp left, turn right into Mill Lane, a public bridleway, signposted Nottingham canal. 100 yards along this track turn left, at the footpath sign and stile, and cross the field to the Nottingham Canal. Cross it and turn left and walk along the tow path with the canal on your immediate left. Follow the canal for the next 2½ miles. Pass under the A609 road and M1 before reaching Swansea Bridge. Cross the bridge and bear left as signposted, and walk around Swansea Houses back to the canal. Shortly afterwards turn right and leave the canal and cross the railway line and two fields to the A6007, Ilkeston Road, at New Stapleford. Turn right then left shortly afterwards along Pasture Road. Take the first road on your right—Morebridge Lane—and follow this to Stanton Gate and the Erewash Canal, ½ mile away.

Turn right and walk beside the Erewash Canal for the next 4½ miles to the Bridge Inn at Cotmanhay. First you walk past Stanton and Staveley works and junction of the Nutbrook Canal, which is now filled in. At Ilkeston you reach the Gallows Inn and lock. Just over two miles later your first Bridge Inn and a little over ½ mile brings you to the Bridge Inn at Cotmanhay. Inbetween these two inns on your right is the impressive Bennerley Viaduct built in 1878; now a Grade 2 listed building. At the Inn turn right along a track which soon swings left before crossing the railway line. Beyond cross a footbridge over the Erewash river and after a few concrete slabs bear right and follow the distinct path close to the field boundary on your right. After ¼ mile gain a works road and walk along it to the first lefthand bend.

On your right is a stile and path to Awsworth. After the first field you enter a track and the first sign of the Nottingham Canal, now all filled in but the bridge gives it away. Turn right as footpath signposted across a playing field then an overgrown field to railway arch, footpath sign,and stile beside Napthen House (boarding kennels). Turn right then left as footpath signposted and gain the Nottingham canal. For the next 1½ miles you follow the line of the canal. First crossing the Awsworth road, then the A6096 road at Cossal Marsh and just over ½ mile later turn left across the filled in canal, into Mill Lane, which you walked part of at the beginning. Walk along the track to the stile and path you used on starting. Turn left over the stile and cross the field to the top, to the road at Cossall. Turn right along it past the almshouses to the car park.

EREWASH CANAL— WALK 4—*SANDIACRE*—3 miles

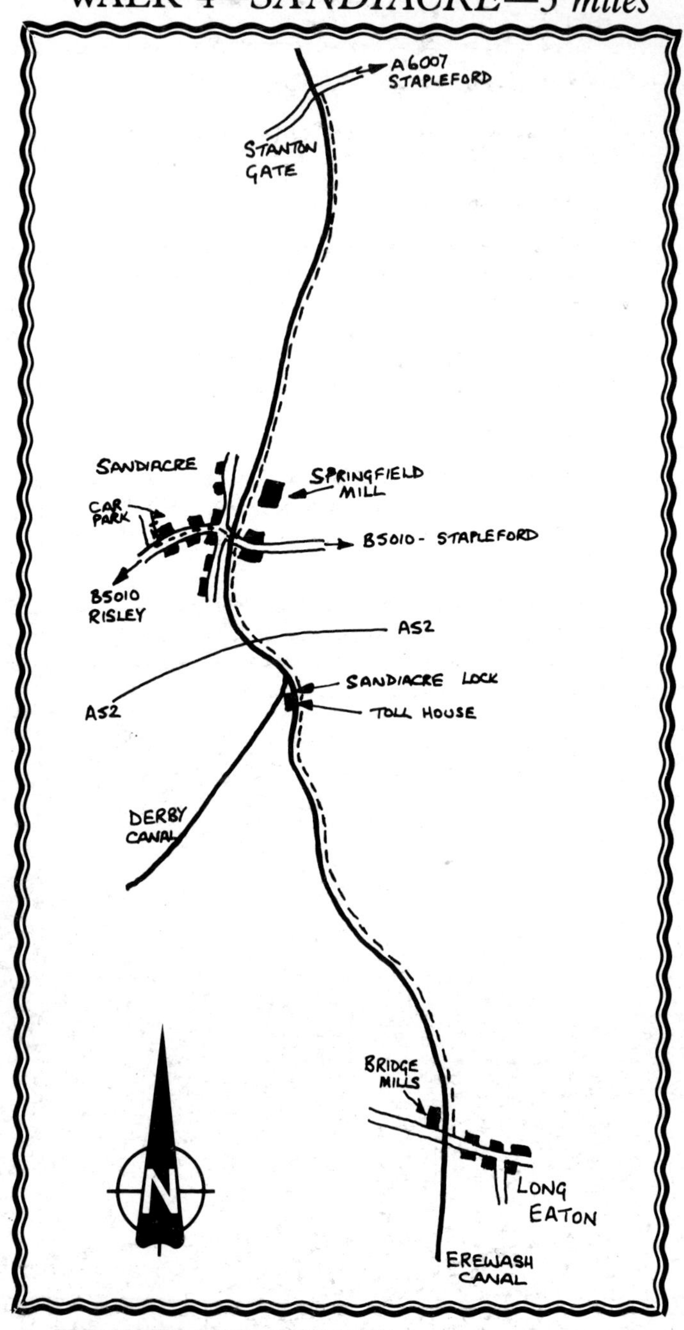

EREWASH CANAL— WALK 5—*SANDIACRE*—4 miles

EREWASH CANAL—WALKS 4 and 5—
3 AND 4 miles—*allow 1½ hours*

ROUTE—*Sandiacre—Erewash Canal—Sandiacre.*

MAPS—*O.S. 1:50,000 Sheet No. 129—Nottingham and Loughborough—*
O.S. 1:25,000 Sheet No. SK 43/53—Nottingham (South West)

CAR PARK—*Bennett Street.*

ABOUT THE WALKS—Sandiacre is ideally placed with some of the most attractive canal walking to the north and south of the town. To the north is the Springfield Mill and southwards the junction of the Derby and Erewash Canals, close to the only toll house on the Erewash Canal. Because of the built up area either side of the canals, both these short walks return the same way. The southern walk to Long Eaton can be used with Walk No. 6 to make a long walk to Trentlock.

WALKING INSTRUCTIONS

WALK 4—3 miles—north to Stanton Gate. Walk to the main cross roads, beside the Plough Inn, and cross the canal road bridge and turn left. Walk beside the canal past the attractive Springfield Mill, to the first road at Stanton Gate, 1½ miles away. Return same way.

WALK 5—4 miles—south to Long Eaton. Walk to the main cross roads and cross the canal road bridge and turn right onto the canal. Follow the canal for 2 miles, past the Derby canal junction to the A6005 road at Long Eaton, close to the Harrington Arms and Bridge Mills. Return same way.

BRIDGE MILL,
LONG EATON

SPRINGFIELD MILL,
SANDIACRE

EREWASH CANAL—
WALK 6—*TRENTLOCK*—6 miles

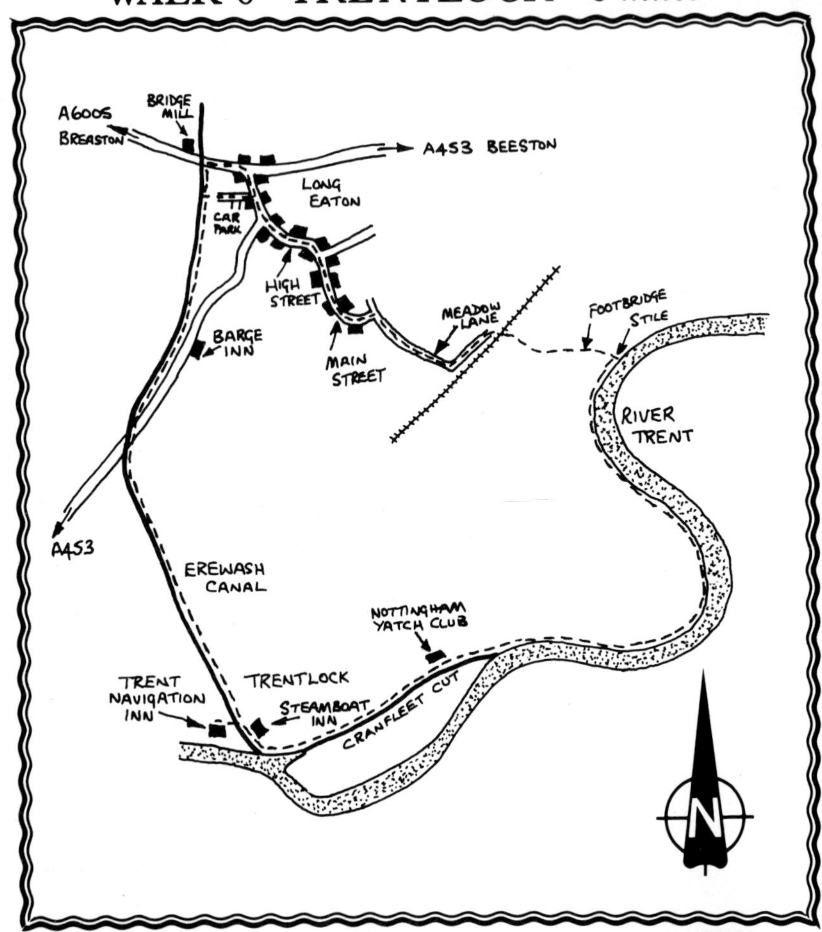

BARGE INN, NR. LONG EATON

EREWASH CANAL—WALK 6—
6 miles—*allow 3 hours*

ROUTE— *Trentlock—River Trent—Long Eaton—Erewash Canal—Trentlock.*

MAPS— *O.S. 1:50,000 Sheet No 129—Nottingham and Loughborough— O.S. 1:25,000 Sheet No SK 43/53—Nottingham (South West)*

CAR PARK— *Trentlock and Long Eaton—Regent Street.*

ABOUT THE WALK— The walk can either be started from Trentlock or Long Eaton. I prefer the former as the road section through Long Eaton linking the Trent and Erewash canal is done at the halfway point, leaving a splendid walk along the canal to the Trent and Steamboat Inn. The walk is along the final section of the Erewash Canal to where it joins the river Trent. You walk beside the river for a little over two miles before walking through Long Eaton to the canal. A really enjoyable walk.

WALKING INSTRUCTIONS— From Trentlock and the Steamboat Inn, keep to the lefthand side of the canal and bear left along the Cranfleet Cut. After a mile reach the Cranfleet Lock by the club house of the Nottingham Yacht Club. Continue along the banks of the navigable river Trent for 1½ miles, as it loops around. The path is well defined and stiled. After a mile you begin passing a large lake on your left and can see ahead a semi-circular footbridge. When almost level with it at a stile leave the river and turn left along the path then bridge. Continue ahead with some earthworks on your left before gaining the top of a small earthwork. Follow this round towards your right to a stile and footpath sign, beside the railway—Attenborough. At the lane beyond turn left along it—Barton Road—and enter the outskirts of Long Eaton.

At the end turn right into Meadow Lane and pass under the railway. Shortly afterwards bear left over another railway line and into Main Street. Follow this past the Victoria Inn and into High Street and the main shopping area of Long Eaton. Pass the Royal Inn, a Berni steak house, and onto the Market Place and St. Laurence church. To your left is Regent Street and car park. At the main road—A6005—turn left along it and just before the Harrington Arms and Bridge Mills, descend to the Erewash Canal. Walk beside the canal for just over 2 miles back to Trentlock.

CRANFLEET CUT

*LANGLEY MILL BASIN,
MILEAGE PLAQUE*

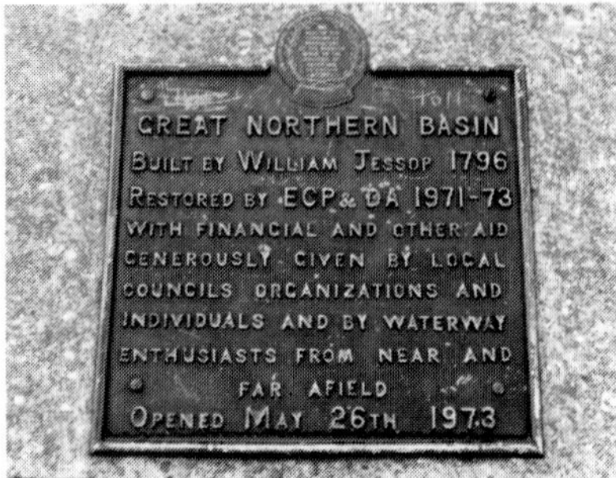

*GREAT NORTHERN
BASIN PLAQUE*

THE BRIDGE INN, EREWASH CANAL

STEAMBOAT INN, TRENTLOCK

EREWASH CANAL—WALK 7—
11½ miles (23 miles)—*allow 5 hours*

ROUTE—*Erewash Canal from end to end—Great Northern Basin to Trentlock.*

MAPS—*1:50,000 Sheet 129—Nottingham and Loughborough —1:25,000 Sheet SK 44/54—Nottingham (North) and Ilkeston —1:25,000 Sheet SK 43/53—Nottingham (South West)*

CAR PARKS—*Northern end—Langley Mill/Great Northern Basin —Southern end—Trentlock*

ABOUT THE WALK—Possibly the finest canal walk in the area as you walk from the Great Northern Basin at Langley Mill, along the whole length of Erewash Canal, to its junction with the river Trent at Trentlock. You can do it as a return walk—23 miles—about 8/9 hours of walking. On the way you see a wealth of historical features, narrowboats cruising on the water, past locks and old canal junctions, through differing countryside and landscape and past at least seven inns—in the early part, one a mile! The canal is a popular fishing area with gudgeon, roach, carp, tench and bream.

NUTBROOK CANAL

Authorised in 1793 and opened in 1795. Built by Benjamin Outram at a cost of £22,800.

The canal was 4½ miles long and linked the collieries at Shipley and West Hallam with the Erewash Canal at Stanton, via Kirk Hallam. There were three reservoirs at Shipley to feed the canal, two of which remain today. Along its length were 13 locks. Mining subsidence involved expensive repairs to the canal leading to its abandonment and by 1890 it was little used. In 1948 Stanton and Staveley aquired it and their factory straddles the site of the canal and the Erewash connection is filled in. A small section west of the factory towards Kirk Hallam is full of water and can be traced. Beyond Kirk Hallam little remains.

DALE

Abbey—completed in late 13th century and was dissolved in 1539. Little remains today except for the solitary window arch—40 feet high by 16 feet wide. The stained glass windows were removed and are now in the north aisle of Morley church, four miles away, and are particularly fine.

Church—shares the same roof as the adjoining farm and its present form dates from 1480. Inside it measures 26 feet by 25 feet and the 15th century abbey font is here. The farmhouse was at one time an inn.

Hermit's Cave—the shallow cave with door and two windows was carved by a hermit between 1130—1140 A.D.

NUTBROOK CANAL—
WALK 1—*STANTON BY DALE—7 miles*

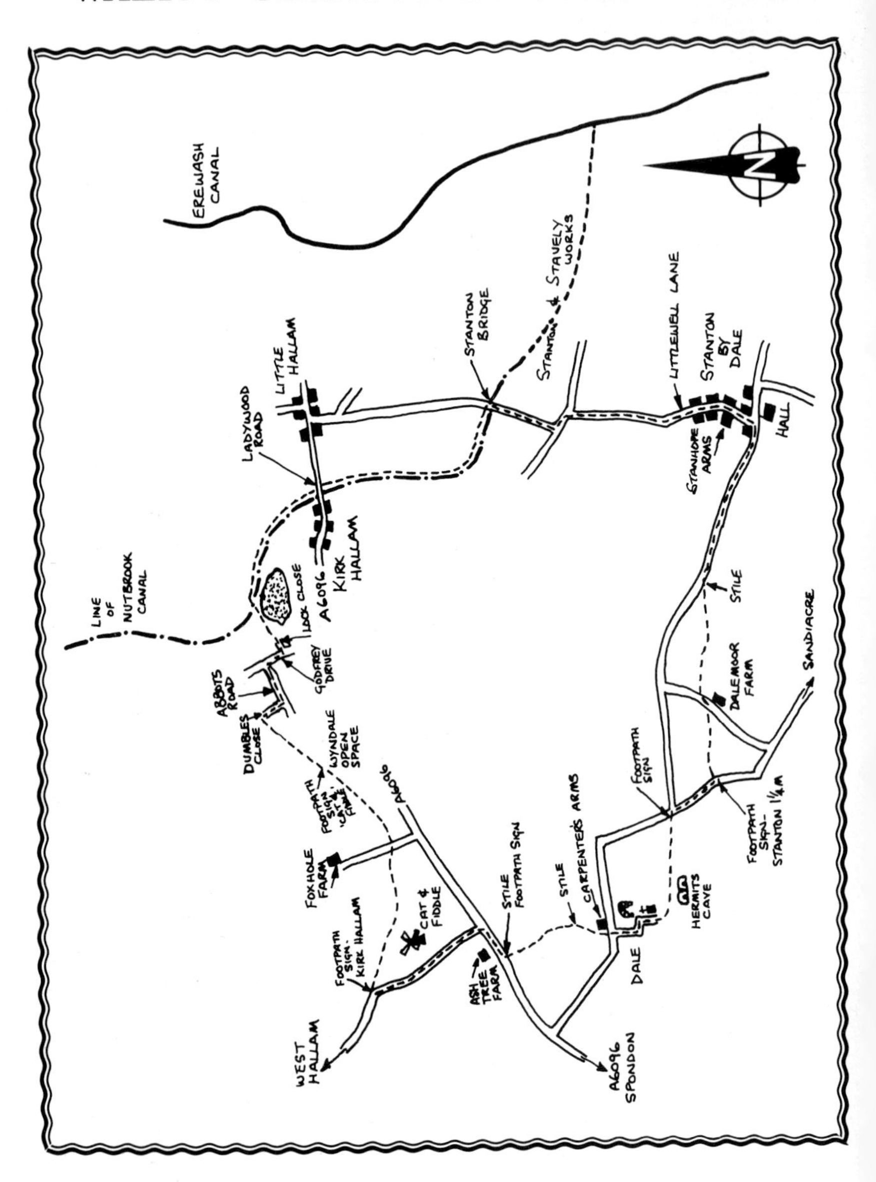

There is a path soon on your left which will lead you into Stanton near its church, but by walking on the road you are able to see more of Stanton, including its hall, cross and waterpump.Entering the village turn left and descend the road—Littlewell Lane—past the Stanhope Arms and into Stanton & Staveley works. After crossing the railway line at the road junction beyond turn left and right shortly afterwards. This road returns you to the Nutbrook Canal and the walk's starting point.

NUTBROOK CANAL—7 miles—*allow 3 hours*

ROUTE—*Nutbrook Canal—Kirk Hallam—Cat & Fiddle—Dale—Stanton by Dale—Nutbrook Canal.*

MAPS—*1:50,000 Sheet 129—Nottingham and Loughborough —1:25,000 Sheet SK 44/54—Nottingham (North) and Ilkeston —1:25,000 Sheet SK 43/53—Nottingham (South West)*

CAR PARK—*No official one, but parking space beside road at Nutbrook Canal.*

ABOUT THE WALK—First you follow all that is left of the Nutbrook Canal before crossing the fields to Dale. Dale is one of my favourite places of Derbyshire, being so rich in history with church, windmill, ruined abbey and a hermits cave. To regain your starting point you cross further fields to Stanton by Dale and a mile of road walking through Stanton and Staveley Works, which straddles the site of the Nutbrook Canal, returns you to the canal.

WALKING INSTRUCTIONS—From Stanton Bridge on the Stanton to Little Hallam road, pass through the metal bollard stile and walk along the path with the canal on your left. Follow it as it curves right through some trees before passing under a bridge. ¼ mile later as you get near to Kirk Hallam cross a small footbridge. Do not follow the path to your left over the playing field, but keep ahead on an ill defined path close to the canal remains and Nut Brook. 200 yards later gain the A6096 road. Go straight across (Ladywood Road) and continue following the indistinct path close to the brook and canal remains. After ½ mile reach a lake on your left and clear canal remains. A little further to your right are further well preserved remains—the last of the canal. Turn left on the tarmaced path to Lock Close and then right into Godfrey Drive. Turn left into Abbot Road and right into Dumbles Close. At House No 35 follow the path through the estate to Wyndale Open Space. There on the lefthandside is the path sign for the Cat & Fiddle. The path keeps to the field edge and is well stiled and after ½ mile comes near the A6096 road. Here the path bears right with the windmill prominently on the hill on your left. After 200 yards you descend a hedged track to road, beside footpath sign—Kirk Hallam.

Turn left and ascend Cat & Fiddle Lane. At the main road, A6096, turn right and almost opposite Ashtree Farm, descend to stile and footpath sign. Descend field to track, which cross directly, and continue through next field to footbridge. Over this bear right to Carpenter's Arms. Descend road beyond into Dale following the road past the church on your left, dedicated to All Saints. Continue past the farm now on a bridleway as you bear left on a wide path past the Hermits Cave on your right. Pass through gate and across the field to stile and footpath sign. Turn right up the road and after 100 yards left at the stile and footpath sign-Stanton 1¼ miles. The path line is indistinct but well stiled and at the end of the third field gain a gate before the road, with Dalesmoor Farm opposite to your right. Turn left along the road to the first gate on your right. Pass through a stile beyond before crossing the field to another stile and the righthand side of a small plantation. Walk beside it on your left to a gate and descend to a stile and road to Stanton by Dale. On your right is a small lake.

NUTBROOK CANAL

CROSS, STANTON BY DALE

DERBY CANAL

Authorised on May 7th 1793 and engineered by Benjamin Outram. It was opened in 1796 and had cost £100,000.

The canal was 14½ miles long from the Erewash Canal, south of Sandiacre to the Trent and Mersey Canal at Swarkestone. En route passing through Breaston, Borrowash, Spondon, Derby and Chellaston. There were nine locks and in Derby crossed the River Derwent above a 300 foot weir. The towpath was a wooden footbridge, known as Long Horse-Bridge, and was demolished in 1959. There were three branches; one via White Bear Lock in Derby, rose through Phoenix Lock to the River Derwent, which was navigable for 1½ miles to Darley Mills. Another went to Little Eaton, where the 'gang road', a tramroad, led to Denby colleries.

Derby was a major inland port with four large basins. Here the canal was carried across Mill Fleam in the first metal trough (aqueduct) in the country. It was made at Butterley Ironworks in 1795, in five sections—6 foot deep, 8 foot long at the top, and 9 foot long at the bottom and overall 2 inches thick. The five sections were bolted together.

The Derby Canal Company was privately owned and was never a hugely successful canal because of its high construction costs. It was never nationalised and in 1964 was abandoned. Much of it has been filled in and almost lost, but some sections can still be traced. At the beginning of this century it was little used and after 1935 hardly at all. In its heyday it was popular, and goods arriving at Liverpool started their canal journey at Runcorn Gap and reached Derby six days later. On Market day a market boat left Swarkestone for Derby, carrying passengers—

> *"...a market boat, decked over, with seats, and a fire-place, for the accommodation of passengers, starts from Swarkestone every Friday morning, to carry market people to Derby, at 6d each; which again leaves Derby at 4 o'clock for Swarkestone."*
>
> **J. Farey,** A General View of the Agriculture of Derbyshire, 1817.

SANDIACRE LOCK AND TOLL HOUSE

DERBY CANAL— WALK 1—*LONG EATON—9 miles*

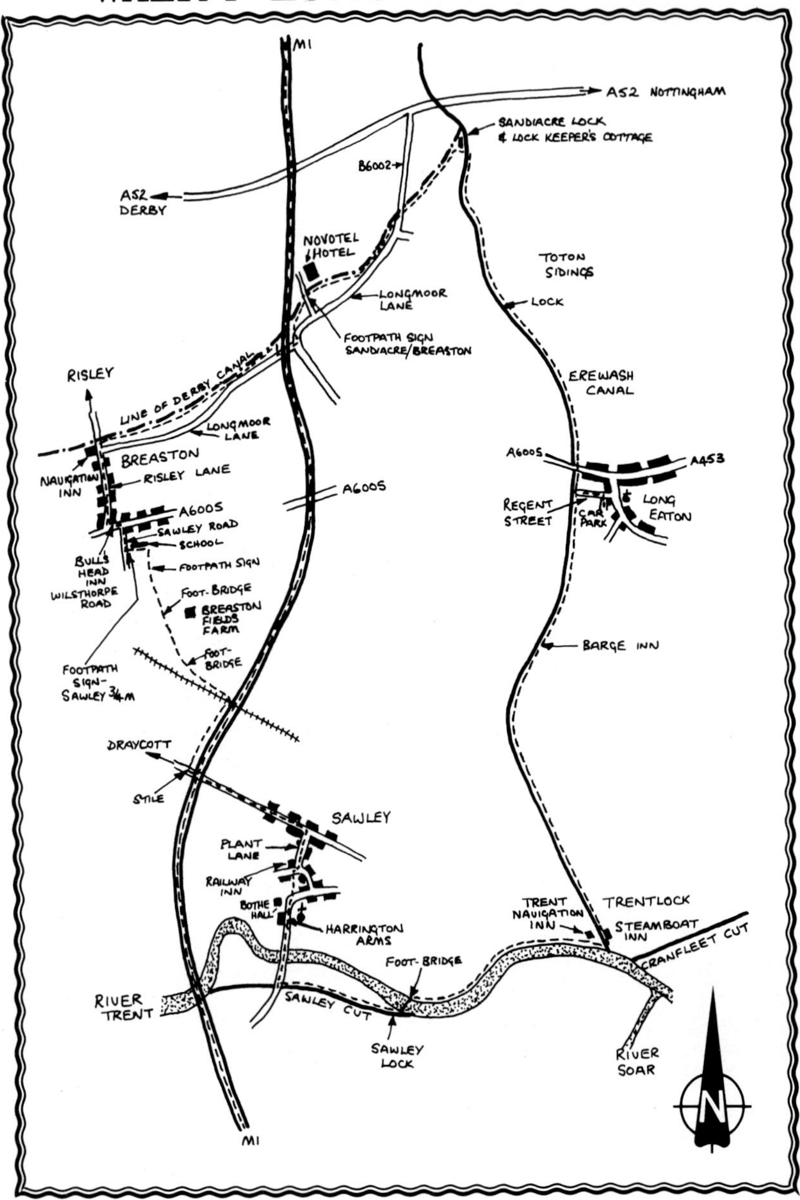

Keep the Sawley Bridge Marina on your right, across the water and follow the tarmaced road to Sawley Lock. Just beyond ascend the footbridge over the River Trent and turn right, along the path along the banks of the river. A mile later reach Trentlock, with the Trent Navigation Inn on your left, before reaching the Erewash Canal. Cross over the canal and turn left along the towpath past the Steamboat Inn. Follow the towpath for the next 2½ miles back to Long Eaton. As you near the Bridge Mills, turn right into Regent Street and retrace your steps back to the car park.

DERBY CANAL—WALK 1—
9 miles—*allow 4 hours*

ROUTE—*Long Eaton—Erewash Canal—Sandiacre Lock—Derby Canal—Breaston—Sawley—Sawley Cut—Trentlock—Erewash Canal—Long Eaton.*

MAPS—*1:50,000—Sheet No 129—Nottingham and Loughborough—1:25,000—Sheet No SK 43/53—Nottingham (South West)*

CAR PARKS—*Regent Street, Long Eaton —Trentlock*

ABOUT THE WALK—The walk is a slight misnomer as you will be walking beside three canals. From Long Eaton you follow the Erewash Canal to its junction with the Derby Canal. You follow nearly three miles along the line of this canal before crossing the fields and roads from Breaston to Sawley. Here you walk beside the Sawley Cut on the Trent Navigation and River Trent to Trentlock and the junction with the Erewash Canal. You walk up the canal back to Long Eaton.

WALKING INSTRUCTIONS—From the car park, just off Regent Street, in central Long Eaton, walk back to Regent Street and turn left and follow it to the end, where there is an entrance onto the Erewash Canal. Turn right and walk along the towpath, past the Bridge Mills on your left. Keep on the canal for just over a mile past Dockholme Lock to Sandiacre Lock. Turn left over the bridge, just infront of the canal cottage to the bridge over the Derby Canal. Turn left and follow the distinct path along the line of the Derby Canal. After ¼ mile pass under the B6002 canal road bridge and bear left along the path, with the road close by on your left. After ¼ mile the path bears right away from the road and continue along to the road close to the M1 ahead. On your right is the Novotel Hotel. Cross the road as footpath signposted—Breaston/Sandiacre. Beneath the M1 bear left along the edge of the park to the road bridge under the M1 and pass under it. Turn right immediately over the stile and cross the field to the hedge. Turn left and continue along the line of the Derby Canal.The next mile is very well stiled and much of the walking is between fences wide apart, illustrating the width of the canal.

Upon reaching the road with the Navigation Inn opposite, turn left along Risley Lane and follow it to its junction with the A6005, ¼ mile away, beside the Bulls Head Inn. Turn left and 40 yards later right into Sawley Road. 40 yards later, turn left onto fenced path—signposted Sawley ¾ mile. After 50 yards turn right into a hedged path and follow it to open fields, after crossing a footbridge. Continue ahead across the field to a stile and across the next to a footbridge. Cross the field strip beyond to the farm road to Breaston Fields Farm. The path beyond is unclear and it is simpler to keep to the field edge, first keeping it on your immediate right, heading for the railway line. Cross a footbridge just before the railway and turn left keeping to the field boundary benath the railway. Just before the end of the field, turn right, through the footpath gate and cross the railway line. Continue beside the field boundary on your left, with the M1 above. At the end of the field ascend the stile and turn left along Sawley Road and pass under the M1. Follow the road for ½ mile to Plant Lane on your right. Follow this to the road junction beside the Railway Inn. Turn right and left almost immediately, on the right of House No 54 along the path, to the road—A435—opposite the Sawley Church, with Bothe Hall on your right. Turn right beside the road past the Harrington Arms on your right and over Harrington Bridge over the River Trent. Just beyond reach Sawley Cut and turn left.

DERBY CANAL–
WALK 2–*SWARKESTONE–3½ miles*

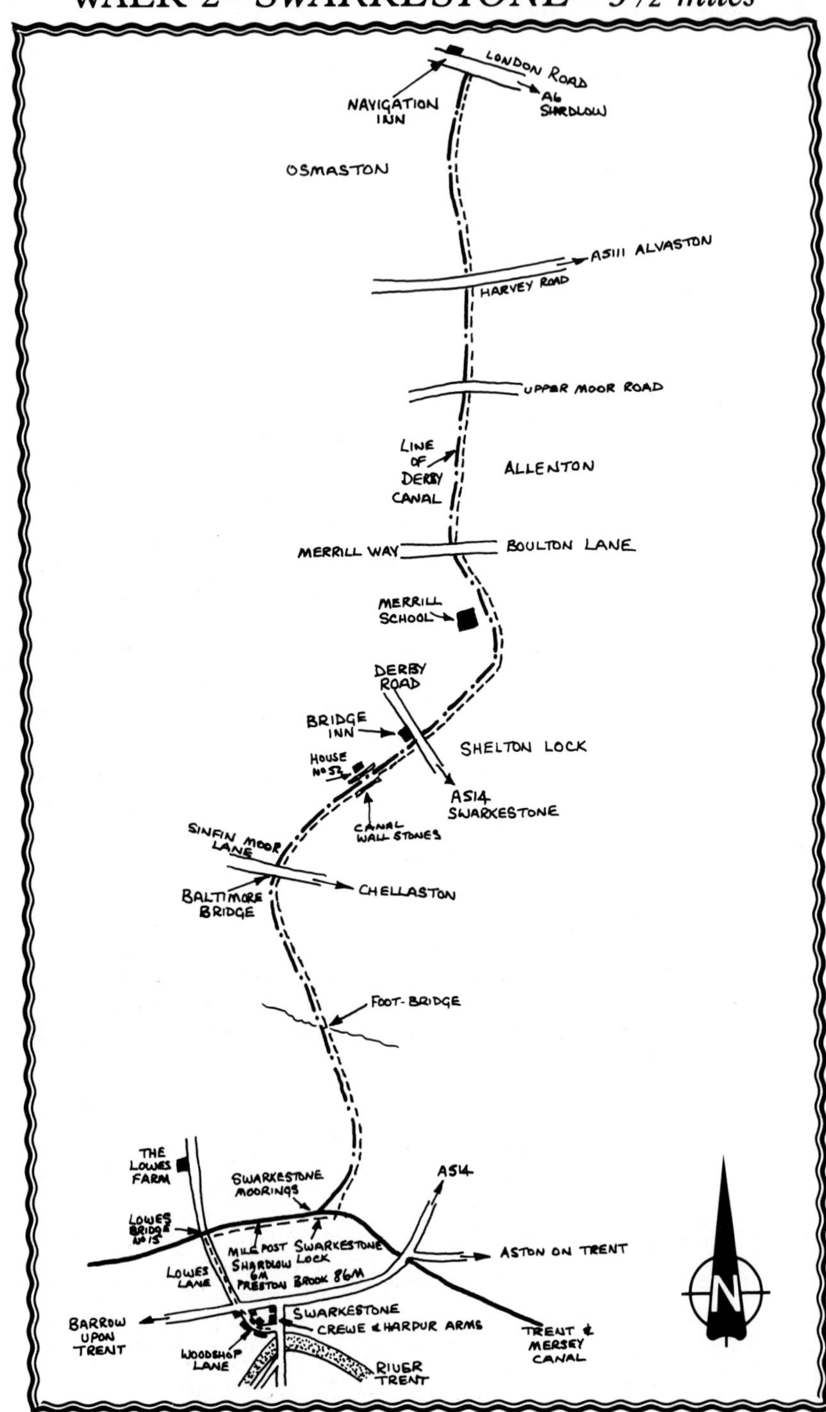

LONDON ROAD
NAVIGATION INN
A6 SHARDLOW
OSMASTON
A5111 ALVASTON
HARVEY ROAD
UPPER MOOR ROAD
LINE OF DERBY CANAL
ALLENTON
MERRILL WAY
BOULTON LANE
MERRILL SCHOOL
DERBY ROAD
BRIDGE INN
SHELTON LOCK
HOUSE No 52
A514 SWARKESTONE
CANAL WALL STONES
SINFIN MOOR LANE
BALTIMORE BRIDGE
CHELLASTON
FOOT-BRIDGE
THE LOWES FARM
SWARKESTONE MOORINGS
A514
LOWES BRIDGE No 15
MILE POST SHARDLOW 6M PRESTON BROOK 86M
SWARKESTONE LOCK
ASTON ON TRENT
LOWES LANE
SWARKESTONE
CREWE & HARPUR ARMS
BARROW UPON TRENT
WOODSHOP LANE
RIVER TRENT
TRENT & MERSEY CANAL
N

DERBY CANAL—WALK 2—
3½ miles one way—*allow 1½ hours*

ROUTE—*Swarkestone—The Lowes Lock—Derby Canal—Shelton Lock—Allenton—Osmaston—A6, Derby.*

MAPS—*1:50,000—Sheet No 128—Derby and Burton Upon Trent—1:25,000—Sheet No SK 22/32—Burton Upon Trent —1:25,000—Sheet No SK 23/33—Derby*

CAR PARK—*No official one, but space on lanes beside the canal—Lowes Lane and near Swarkestone Lock.*

ABOUT THE WALK—From Swarkestone you follow a fragment of the Trent & Mersey Canal to the junction of the now abandoned Derby Canal. Here you follow the line of the canal, at first very discernible to Shelton Lock, before following the basic line of the now filled in canal. Nevertheless an interesting walk into the outskirts of Derby. You can either do it as a one-way walk or return the same way. Swarkestone is worth exploring to see the river Trent and famous Swarkestone Bridge.

WALKING INSTRUCTIONS—From Swarkestone follow Woodshop Lane through the village to the A5132 road. Cross over onto Lowes Lane and follow this over the railway to Lowes Bridge (No 15) over the Trent & Mersey Canal. Turn right at the bridge and descend to the tow path, following for just over ¼ mile. On the way passing canal milepost—Shardlow 6 miles, Preston Brook 86 miles. A little further on the opposite side of the canal is Swarkestone Moorings. At Swarkestone Lock, turn left over the bridge and follow the track to bridge over the Derby Canal; turn right just before it and descend to the tow path. The next mile of the canal is attractive walking, being unspoilt and woodland. After ½ mile cross a footbridge and ½ mile later reach Baltimore Bridge.

From here the canal has been filled in but its line is well defined and you walk along a good path. After ¼ mile pass a housing estate on your left and opposite a block of houses, incorporating house no. 52, can be seen the exposed tops of the canal. Just beyond pass under the A514 road at Shelton Lock, with the Bridge Inn on your left. The path is now very prominent as you enter more built up area with the Merrill School (no relation to me) on your left. Cross the road at Allenton and shortly afterwards keep to your right and follow the canal line over another road before gaining the A5111. Cintinue ahead for another mile through Osmaston to gain the A6 road—London Road. The Navigation Inn is on your left. The canal line can be followed a little bit further but beyond has been demolished by industry. Return the same way back to Swarkestone.

DERBY CANAL START—SWARKESTONE END

BEESTON CANAL–
WALK 1–*ATTENBOROUGH–4½ miles*

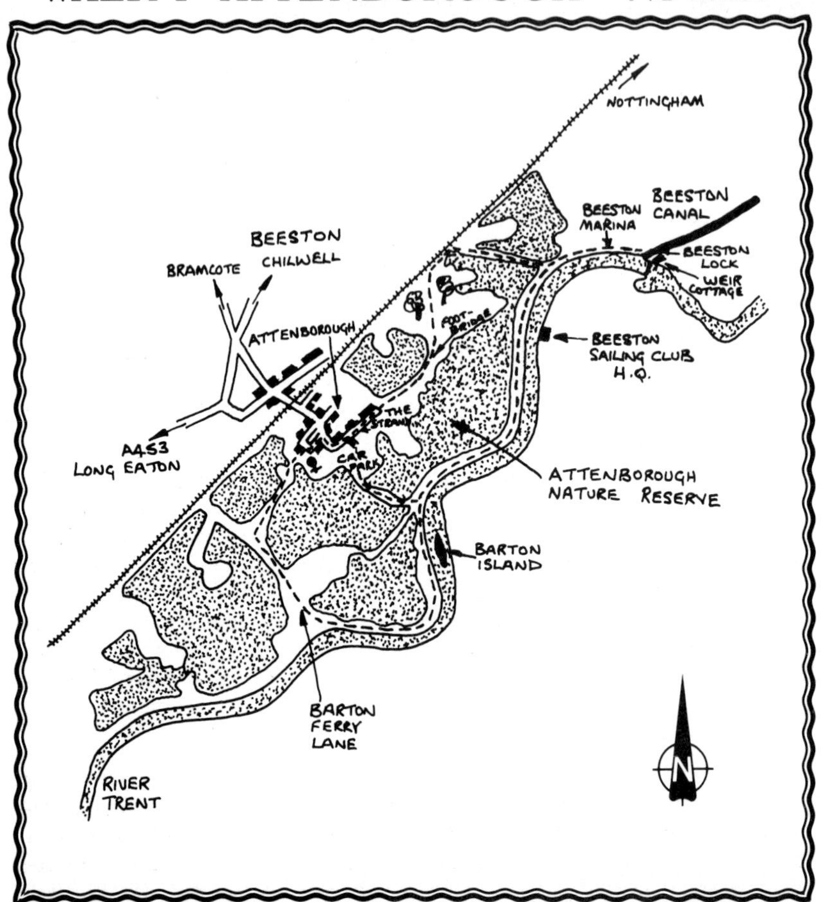

TRENT & RIVER SOAR

BEESTON CANAL–built in 1795 and 2½ miles long from the river Trent to Lenton Chain, where it joined the Nottingham Canal. The River Trent was difficult to pass through at the Wilford Shoals near West Bridgford, and this helped to allieviate the problem. The name Lenton Chain derives from the Trent Navigation Company. From Saturday evening to Monday morning they used to lock the canal by placing a chain across it.

BEESTON CANAL—WALK 1—
4½ miles—*allow 2 hours*

ROUTE—*Attenborough—Nature Reserve—River Trent—Beeston Lock—Nature Reserve—Attenborough.*

MAPS—*1:50,000 Sheet 129—Nottingham and Loughborough —1:25,000 Sheet SK 43/53—Nottingham (South West)*

CAR PARK—*Nature Reserve Car Park, The Strand, Attenborough.*

ABOUT THE WALK—At the beginning and end of the walk you walk through the Attenborough Nature Reserve—old gravel pits—where an amazing variety of birds have been spotted—more than 200 different species. Next you walk beside the navigable River Trent, which links Trentlock with Beeston Lock. At Beeston Lock you can extend the walk by 3 miles (see Beeston Canal Walk 2) by exploring the start of the canal. You return via the gravel pits back to Attenborough. There is no inn on this walk—sorry!

WALKING INSTRUCTIONS—From the car park walk back to the road, The Strand, and follow it round to your left to Church Lane. Turn left along this past the parish church, dedicated to St. Mary the Virgin. Just beyond at the entrance to Ireton House, turn left as bridlepath signed—Barton Ferry Lane ⅓ mile. Walk past the stables on your left and gain a well-used path/track. Follow this between the lakes, over a footbridge to Barton Ferry Lane. Turn left along it—a track—over another bridge and straight ahead to the river Trent, a little over ¼ mile away. Upon reaching the track beside the Trent turn left and walk along the banks of the river for a little over 2 miles. All the time you have the Trent on your right and the lakes of the gravel pits on your left.

Nearing Beeston Lock, on your right on the otherside of the river is Beeston Sailing Club and just ahead you walk through Beeston Marina. Continue to Beeston Lock and Weir Cottage. Here you can do the 3 mile circuit (Beeston Walk 2) or return to Attenborough. To return retrace your steps past the Beeston Marina, before turning right on a path between the lakes, signposted Nature Trail. Just over ¼ mile later near the railway line turn left, as signposted—Nature Trail. The path soon bears left through woodland before crossing a footbridge and walking between more lakes. Walk into The Strand road and follow it back to the car park.

ATTENBOROUGH GRAVEL PITS

The pits are owned by Batterley Aggregates and are jointly managed with the Nottinhamshire Trust for Nature Conservation. The area is mostly reed beds and open water and is a popular bird watching area, with 217 species recorded with many migratory birds passing through, including spoonbill and little crake. Waterfowl are predominant and all year round can be seen, reed bunting, tufted duck, pochard, teal, grebe, shoveler, great crested grebe, little grebe, mallard, moorhen, snipe and numerous gulls.

BEESTON CANAL—
WALK 2—*BEESTON LOCK—3 miles*

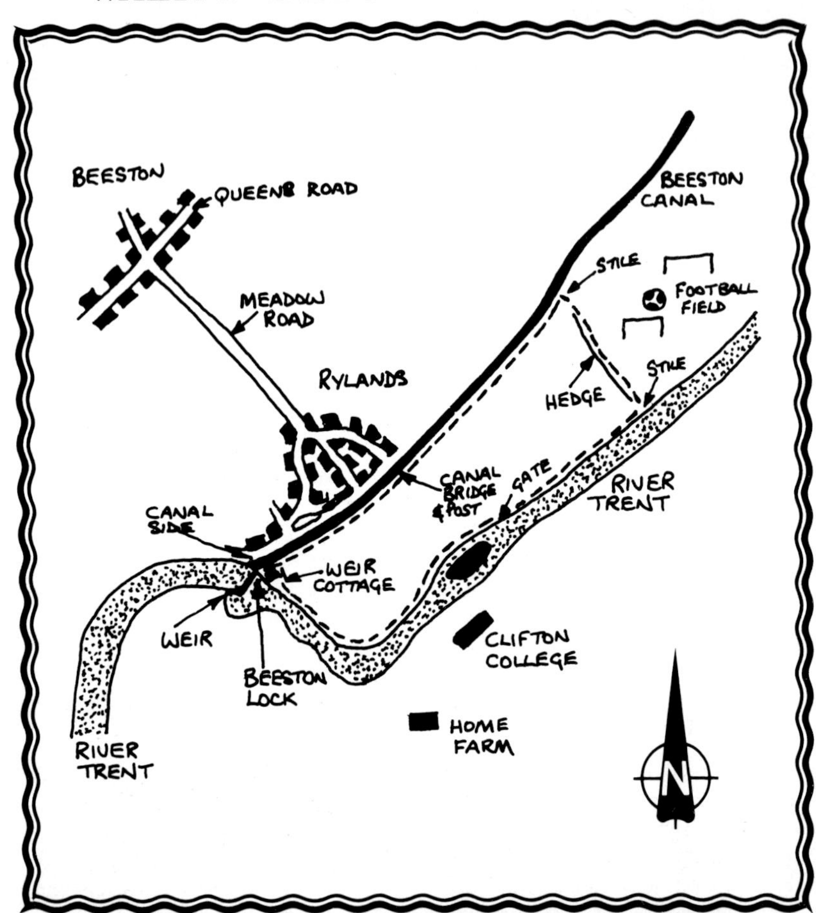

NOTTINGHAM & BEESTON CANAL PLAQUE

BEESTON CANAL—WALK 2—
3 miles—*allow 1½ hours*

ROUTE—*Beeston Lock—River Trent—Beeston Canal—Beeston Lock*

MAPS—*1:50,000 Sheet 129—Nottingham and Loughborough—1:25,000 Sheet SK 43/53—Nottingham (South West)*

CAR PARK—*No official one, but parking space at Beeston Lock on Canal Side road.*

ABOUT THE WALK—A short circular walk around the early part of the canal, first beside the river Trent to see the impressive weir before crossing the field to the Beeston Canal. This walk can be added to Beeston Canal Walk 1.

WALK INSTRUCTIONS—Cross Beeston Lock via footbridge, with Weir Cottage on right, and cross subsequent footbridge and turn right heading for the banks of the river Trent. Follow the defined path for 1¼ miles as you walk above the river past Cherry Island at the midway point. ½ mile later reach a stile and once over this turn left keeping to the field edge, as signposted, with the football field on your right. At the end of the field turn left along the track to a stile and continue beside the Beeston Canal on the other side of the concrete wall on your right. At the first canal bridge, which has rope grooves on the pillars, you gain the canal proper and follow it back to Beeston Lock.

BEESTON LOCK

BEESTON CANAL—
WALK 3—*NOTTINGHAM—4½ miles*

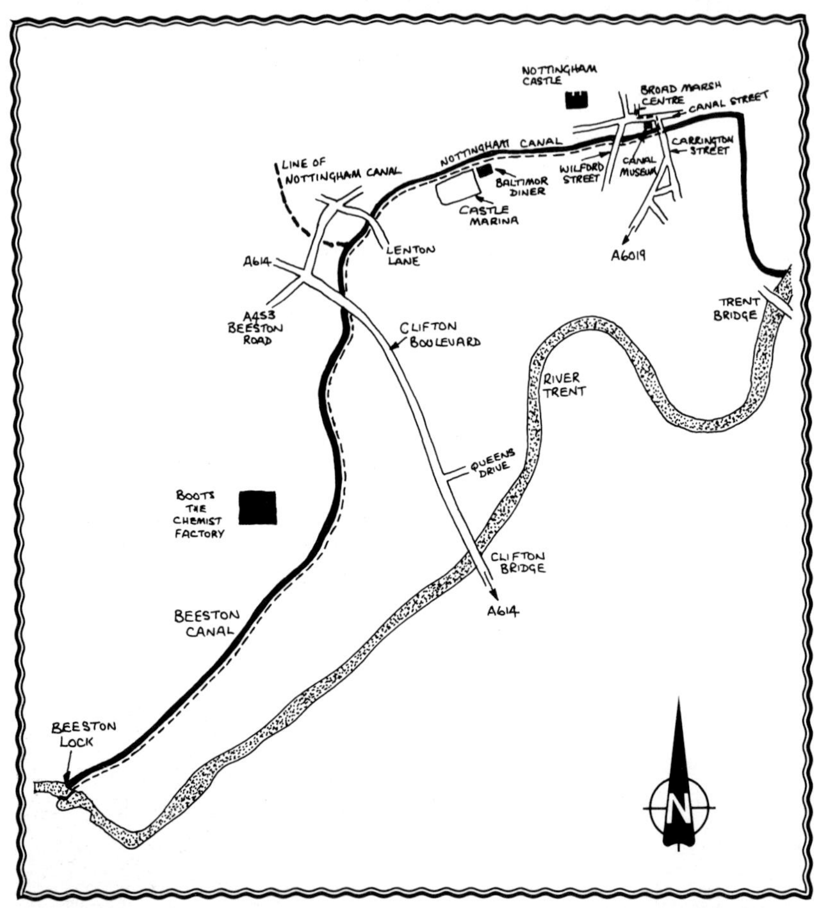

BEESTON MARINA

BEESTON CANAL—WALK 3—
$4\frac{1}{2}$ miles (9 miles round trip)—*allow 2 or 4 hours.*

ROUTE—*Canal Museum, Canal Street, Nottingham—Nottingham/Beeston Canal to Beeston Lock. Return same way.*

MAPS—*1:50,000 Sheet 129—Nottingham and Loughborough —1:25,000 Sheet SK 43/53—Nottingham (South West)*

CAR PARK—*Broadmarsh Centre, Nottingham —Canal Side, Beeston Lock*

ABOUT THE WALK—A very pleasant walk from the Canal Museum in Nottingham along the length of Nottingham/Beeston Canal to its end at Beeston Lock beside the river Trent. You can either do it as a oneway walk or return the same way. The latter I fully recommend for it is surprising how different everything looks from the opposite direction. A visit to the Canal Museum is well worthwhile and gives you greater appreciation and insight into canals and their construction.

WALKING INSTRUCTIONS—From the Canal Museum on Canal Street, turn right, and right again 20 yards later into Carrington Street. 30 yards later turn right, as Canal Towpath signed, and descend to the canal. You keep the canal on your righthand side all the way to Beeston Lock. In the early part you pass the Baltimore Diner on your left and Castle Marina. A mile later you leave the buildings behind for a mile and pass the location of Lenton Chain where the Nottingham Canal from Langley Mill came in. You now continue beside the Beeston Canal for $2\frac{1}{2}$ miles to Beeston Lock. Return the same way. You can do the walk starting from either end.

CANAL MUSEUM, NOTTINGHAM

NOTTINGHAM CANAL—
WALK 1—*NOTTINGHAM—3 miles*

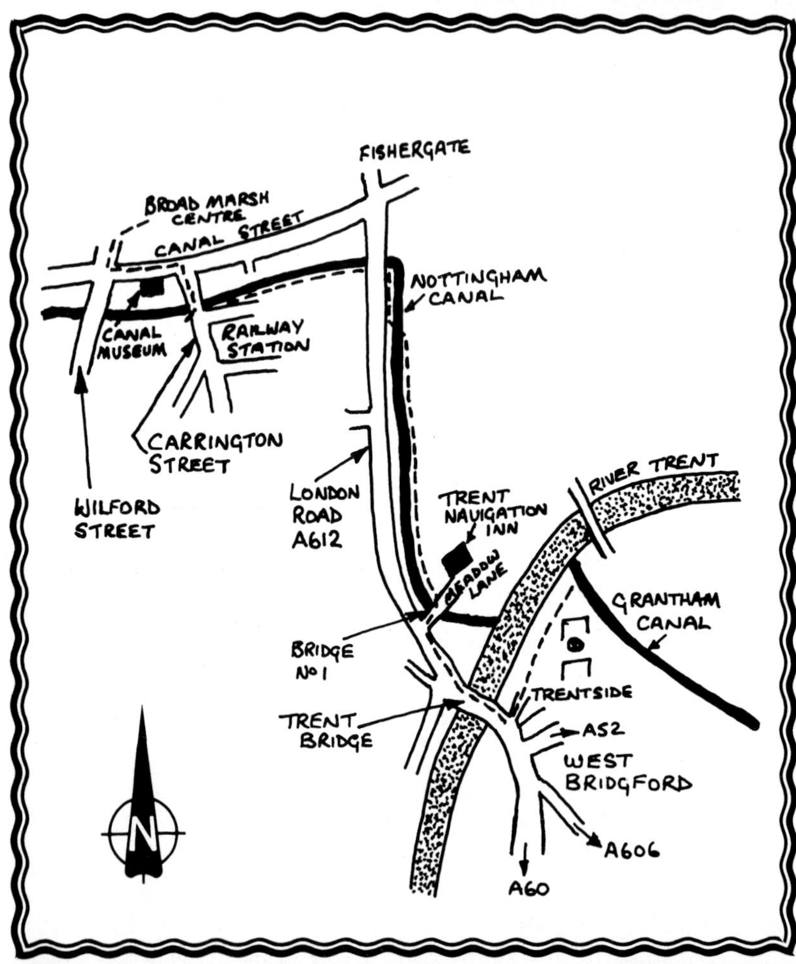

CROSS OVER BRIDGE—NOTTINGHAM

NOTTINGHAM CANAL—WALK 1—
3 miles—*allow 1½ hours*

ROUTE—*Nottingham Canal Museum—Nottingham Canal—Trent Bridge—Grantham Canal—Trent Bridge—Nottingham Canal—Canal Museum.*

MAPS—*1:50,000 Sheet 129—Nottingham and Loughborough —1:25,000 Sheet SK 43/53—Nottingham (South West)*

CAR PARK—*Broadmarsh Centre, Nottingham.*

ABOUT THE WALK—In many ways this is an ideal walk to familiarise yourself with canal walking and the canals detailed in this book. First a visit to the Nottingham Canal Museum explains the canals and their story in the area, together with exhibits and numerous photographs. Next you explore a short section of the Nottingham Canal to where it joins the River Trent. Close by is the Trent Navigation Inn. After crossing Trent Bridge you walk beside the river to see where the Grantham Canal left the river. You return the same way.

WALKING INSTRUCTIONS—From the Canal Museum, turn right along Canal Street for 20 yards and turn right into Carrington Street. 30 yards up here turn right as Canal Towpath signed, and at the canal turn right, and follow the towpath on the righthand side of the canal. You follow it between the tall buildings to the sign opposite—saying Lincoln, Gainsborough and the North. Follow the towpath to your right and soon ascend a footbridge and descend to the towpath on the lefthand side of the canal. Continue along the canal side for a little over ½ mile to Bridge No 1. You can walk a little further but have to return to here. Ascend to Meadow Lane and on your right is the Trent Navigation Inn. Turn left to London Road and turn left along it over Trent Bridge. Just across turn left into Trentside and follow the tarmaced road above the river and past Nottingham Forest Football ground on your right. On your left across the river you can see where the Nottingham canal enters the Trent. Continue ahead a little further to see where the disused Grantham canal leaves the Trent. Retrace your steps back to the Museum and car park opposite.

NOTTINGHAM CANAL

Authorised in 1792. Engineer William Jessop. Opened in 1796 at a cost of £80,000.

The canal was 14⅜ miles long from Langley Mill to the River Trent at Nottingham. There were seven short branches of which the Robinetts branch is one. There were 20 locks including a flight of 14 at Wollaton. Over the B6007 road near Cossall was a single arch aqueduct; today the canal flows through two large pipes. Connected to the Beeston Canal at Lenton Chain.

In 1808—269,456 tons of coal was carried on the Cromford, Erewash and Nottingham canals.

In 1835 the canal was bought by the Ambergate Railway Company. The section from Langley Mill to Lenton Chain ceased to carry any traffic in 1928 and was abandoned nine years later in 1937. The section from Lenton Chain to Nottingham and River Trent, together with the Beeston Canal, is still in use today.

DERBY, EREWASH AND TRENT & MERSEY CANALS

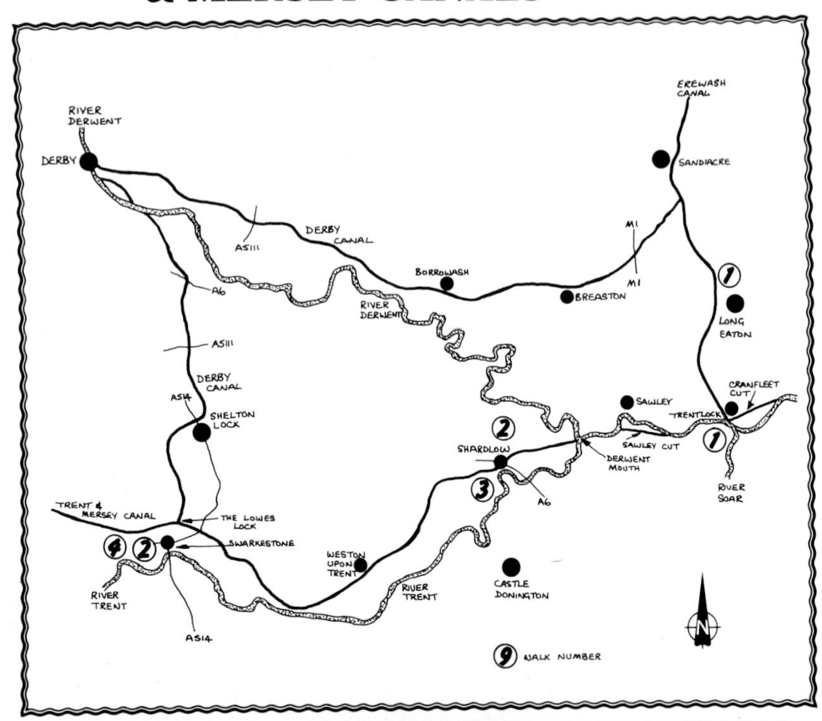

CANAL MILEPOST, SHARDLOW

TRENT & MERSEY CANAL

The River Trent had already been navigable to Burton under an Act of 1699. In 1712 4,000 tons of cheese was transported on the river and 1721 the first boat up the Derwent reached Derby, carrying 'Dale-Boards, tobacco, fish and other merchandise.' A canal linking the river Trent to the Mersey was proposed by Erasmus Darwin and Josiah Wedgwood who saw it as a need for the Potteries and Midlands area. James Brindley surveyed the route and it ran from the Derwent Mouth on the Trent to Preston Brook on the Bridgewater Canal near Runcorn—93⅜ miles. En route passing through Burton-on-Trent, close to Lichfield, before passing through Rugely, Stoke and Middlewich to Preston Brook.

The canal—first known as Grand Trunk—was authorised on 14th May 1766 with a capital of £150,000. Work began on the canal immediately but it was not until 1777 that the whole canal was opened, largely due to the problems of the Harecastle tunnel—2,900 yards long. Many were sceptical that the company would ever pay a dividend but in 1781 5% was paid and in 1825 a £100 share was worth £2,300.

Because of its unique position close to the start of the canal, Shardlow grew into a major inland port. In 1788 the population was 300 and in 1841, 1306. The Trent barges could reach Burton but beyond there the locks were narrow and could only take boats with a seven foot beam. Goods going beyond Burton were transferred to narrow boats in Shardlow and vice versa. It is for this reason that there are numerous warehouses and large buildings beside the canal in Shardlow. Associated industries such as boat-building, crane-building, smithying and rope-making were all carried on here. The clock warehouse, named because of its central clock, dates from 1780 and now houses a museum. Much of the building has been carefully restored and the basin has been returned to its original state. Shardlow is now, justifiably, a conservation area.

CLOCK WAREHOUSE, SHARDLOW

TRENT & MERSEY CANAL– WALK 1–*TRENTLOCK–3 miles*

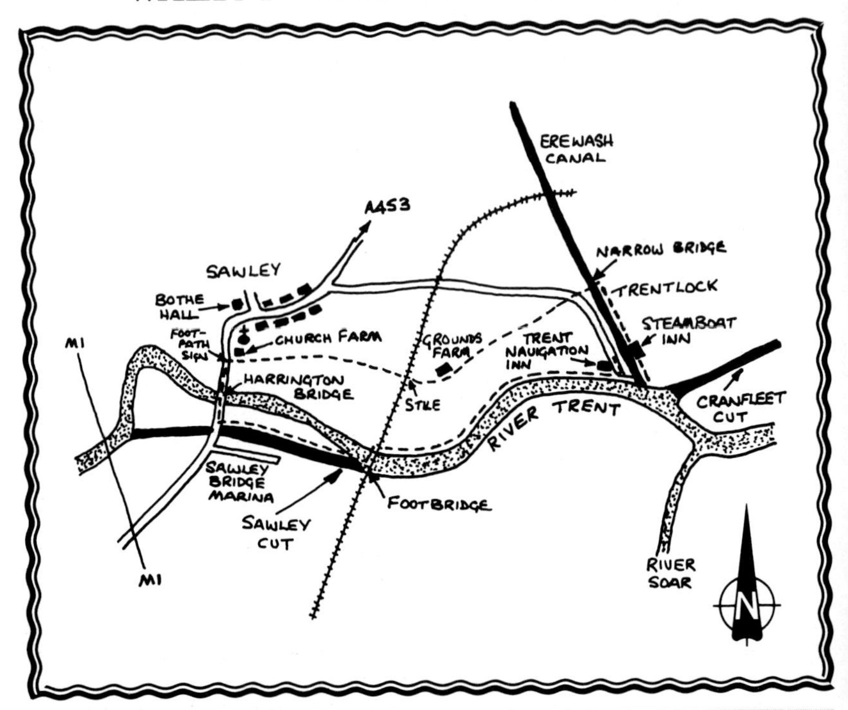

SAWLEY CUT

TRENT & MERSEY CANAL—WALK 1—
3 miles—*allow 1½ hours*

ROUTE— *Trentlock—River Trent—Sawley Cut—Harrington Bridge—Grounds Farm—Trentlock.*

MAPS— *1:50,000—Sheet No 129—Nottingham and Loughborough—1:25,000—Sheet No SK 43/53—Nottingham (South West)*

CAR PARK— *Trentlock*

ABOUT THE WALK—A short walk from the junction of the Erewash Canal with the River Trent/Trent & Mersey Canal, along the banks of the river to Sawley Lock. You return over the fields, with an option to explore the village of Sawley, before doing so.

WALKING INSTRUCTIONS—Turn right out of the car park, past the Trent Navigation Inn to the River Trent and turn right. On your left, a short distance away, is Trentlock and Steamboat Inn. Follow the defined path along the banks of the Trent for a mile to the railway bridge over the Trent. Pass under the arch before turning left and ascending the footbridge over the river. Turn right at the end past Sawley Lock and along the tarmaced road, past the narrow boats and Sawley Bridge Marina on your left. At the road—A453—turn right and walk over Harrington Bridge, over the Trent.

Just before Church Farm on your right, is the footpath sign and stile. If you continue ahead you can explore Sawley and see its church and Bothe Hall. Through the stile the pathline is along a track beside an earth embankment on your right. The river Trent is far to your right. After ½ mile pass under the railway arch and continue ahead for 50 yards to a couple of small ponds. On you left is Grounds Farm. Turn left past the farm keeping the field boundary on your left. After ½ mile reach Lock Lane and cross over to the bridge over the Erewash Canal. Turn right and walk beside the canal to Trentlock and the Steamboat Inn. Cross the canal to the Trent Navigation Inn and retrace your steps back to the car park.

SAWLEY—The church was founded by monks who rowed across the Trent from Repton, in 822. Most of the present building is 14th century with some excellent 15th century oak timbers and carvings. There are several monuments to the Bothe family who founded Bothe Hall opposite in the 15th century. Just up the path on the right of the hall is the house (No 52) where the Rev. John Clifford was born on 16th October 1836. Although only poor he went on to obtain five degrees at London University and became a major Nonconformist.

TRENT & MERSEY CANAL—WALK 2—*SHARDLOW—3 miles*

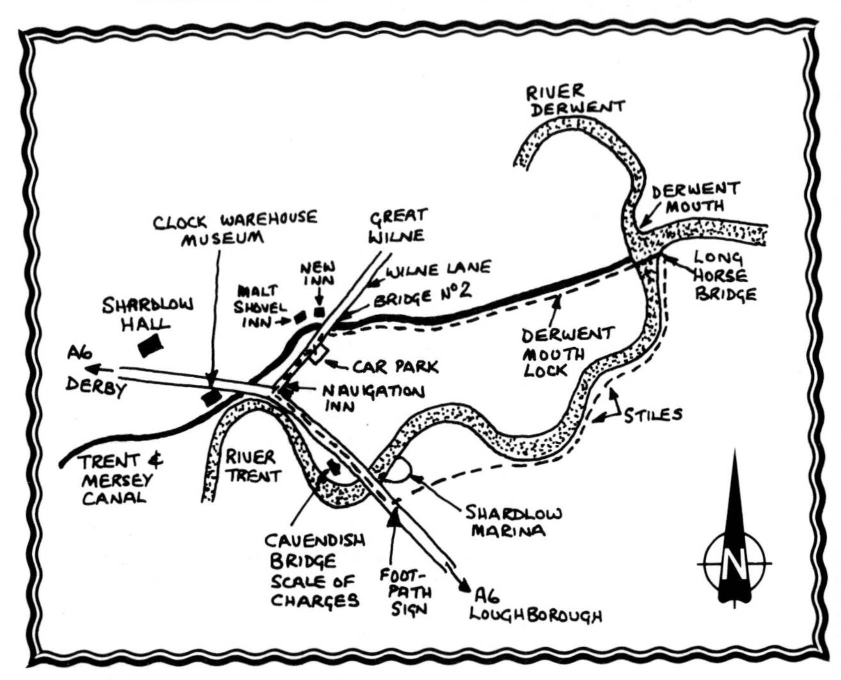

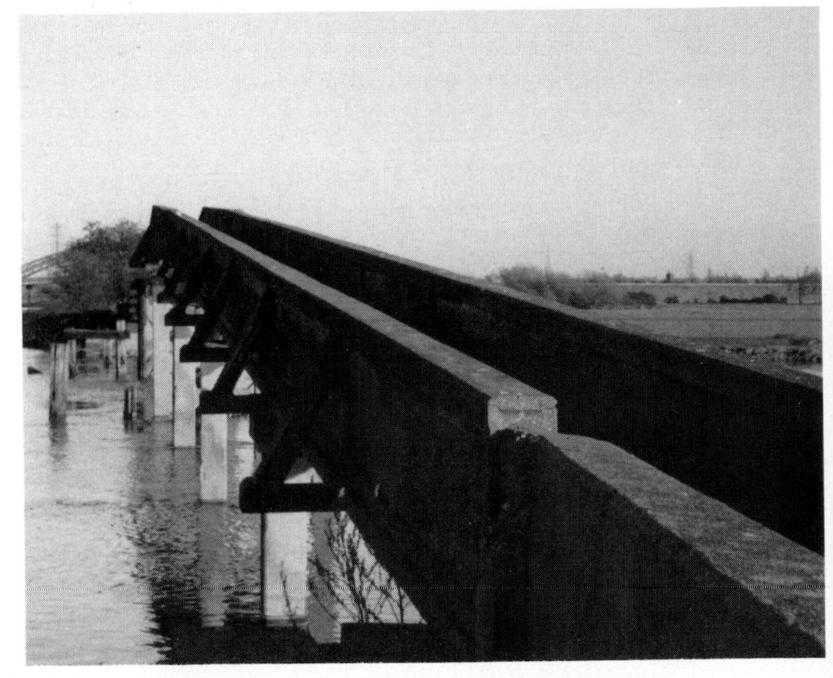

LONG HORSE BRIDGE AT DERWENT MOUTH

TRENT & MERSEY CANAL—WALK 2—
3 MILES—*allow 1½ hours*

ROUTE—*Shardlow—Trent & Mersey Canal—Derwent Mouth—Long Horse Bridge—River Trent—A6—Cavendish Bridge—Shardlow.*

MAPS—*1:50,000—Sheet No 129—Nottingham and Loughborough—1:25,000—Sheet No SK 43/53—Nottingham (South West)*

CAR PARK—*Shardlow, off Wilne Lane*

ABOUT THE WALK—Shardlow is one of the finest and best preserved inland ports in England. This short walk follows the Trent & Mersey canal through Shardlow to the junction of the river Trent and Derwent. You walk beside the Trent back to Shardlow, to explore fully the port and the Canal Museum in the Clock Warehouse.

WALKING INSTRUCTIONS—Turn right out of the car park along Wilne Lane to Bridge No 2 over the canal. Turn left before the bridge and descend to the canal towpath; opposite is the Malt Shovel and New Inn. Turn right and follow the towpath for almost a mile to the rivers Trent and Derwent. After ¾ mile pass the Derwent Mouth Lock. Cross the footbridge over the river Trent (Long Horse Bridge) and turn right. Walk along the banks of the river Trent for almost ¾ mile to where the river turns sharp right. Here continue straight ahead across the field to a stile and footpath sign on the immediate left of a large building complex on your right.

Over the stile gain the A6 road and turn right over the Cavendish Bridge with Shardlow Marina on your right. Continue on into Shardlow, passing the plaque on your left of the scale of charges used on the bridge. Pass the entrance to Wilne Lane and the Navigation Inn to reach the canal. The towpath as signed is on your right, but before following it continue along the A6 to visit the Clock Warehouse on your left. Retrace your steps back to the towpath and walk along it to Bridge No 2 and ascend back to Wilne Lane. Turn right back to the car park.

CAVENDISH BRIDGE TOLLS

TRENT & MERSEY CANAL—WALK 3—*SHARDLOW—5 miles*

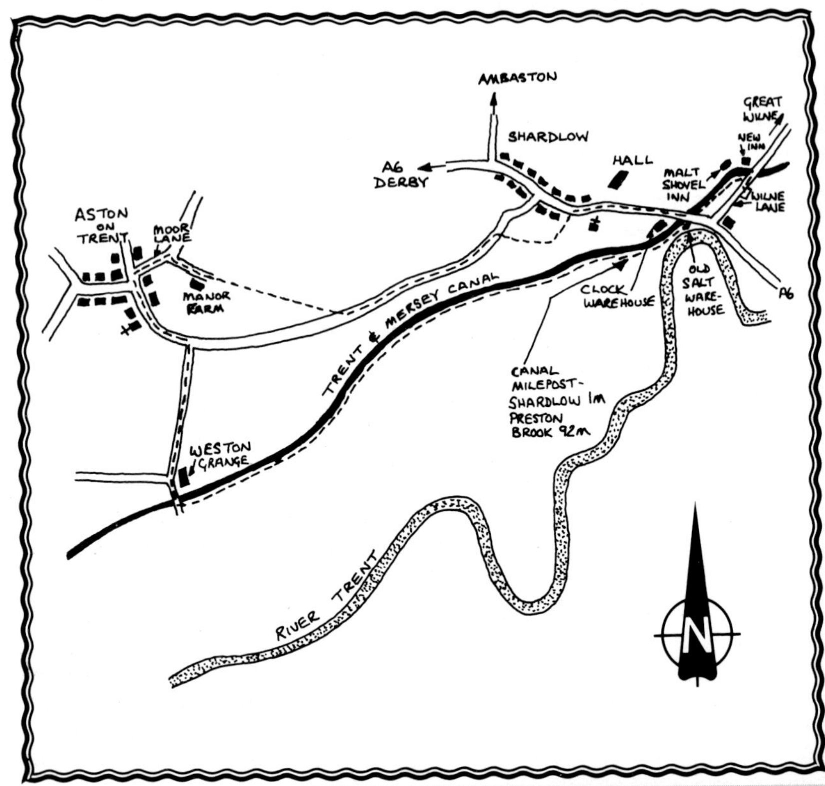

SHARDLOW BASIN

ASTON ON TRENT—All Saints church dates from Norman times but is largely 13th and 15th century. The clerestory is 15th century and the font 13th century.

TRENT & MERSEY CANAL—WALK 3—
5 miles—*allow 3 hours*

ROUTE—*Shardlow—Trent & Mersey Canal—Weston Grange—Aston on Trent—Shardlow.*

MAPS—*1:50,000—Sheet No 129—Nottingham and Loughborough—1:25,000—Sheet SK 43/53—Nottingham (South West) —1:25,000—Sheet SK 42/52—Kegworth*

CAR PARK—*Shardlow—off Wilne Lane*

ABOUT THE WALK—First you explore the canal wharfs and warehouses of Shardlow before following the canal to Weston Grange. You can either return the same way or follow the paths and road to Shardlow via Aston on Trent. The latter gives you the option to explore Shardlow further by seeing its hall and church.

WALKING INSTRUCTIONS—From the car park turn right along Wilne Lane to the bridge (no 2) over the canal. Just before it turn left to the towpath and keep the canal on your righthand side.After a little over ¼ mile reach the A6 road bridge. It is worth ascending to the road, crossing it and descending to the canal again. Where you leave the A6 road, on your right, as recorded on the plaque, is 'The Old Salt Warehouse'. Pass the canal milepost—'Shardlow 1 mile, Preston Brook 92 miles'. On your right is the Clock Warehouse, which incorporates a very interesting Canal Museum and is worth exploring on your return.

Follow the canal for 2½ miles until you reach the fourth bridge over it. Ascend to this and cross to your right to Weston Grange. Just past the building turn right and walk up the lane to Aston on Trent, ½ a mile away. At the road turn left to the church. Beyond at the cross roads, continue ahead and take the second road on your right—'Moor Lane'. Shortly afterwards turn right and follow Manor Farm Road which soon becomes a signposted path, across the fields to the Shardlow road. Turn left and follow the road for ¾ mile to Shardlow. As you enter, turn right onto a path. Keep to the edge of the field, and in the second at the red bricked wall turn left over the footbridge and soon enter central Shardlow and the A6 road. Turn right to pass the church on your right and hall on your left. Continue on the A6 back to the canal, with the Clock Warehouse on your right. Retrace your steps along the canal to your left to the Malt Shovel Inn and Wilne Road car park.

SHARDLOW—was a major inland port, and boats operating in the Derbyshire section of the canal carried up to 40 tons of goods. Until 1785 the boats were hauled by men and from then onwards by horses. There was a stable for 100 horses here and the ropewalk still remains. Shardlow Hall, now an agricultural advisory centre, was built by Leonard Fosbrooke, a carrier, in 1684.

TRENT & MERSEY CANAL

TRENT & MERSEY CANAL— WALK 4—*SWARKESTONE—3½ miles*

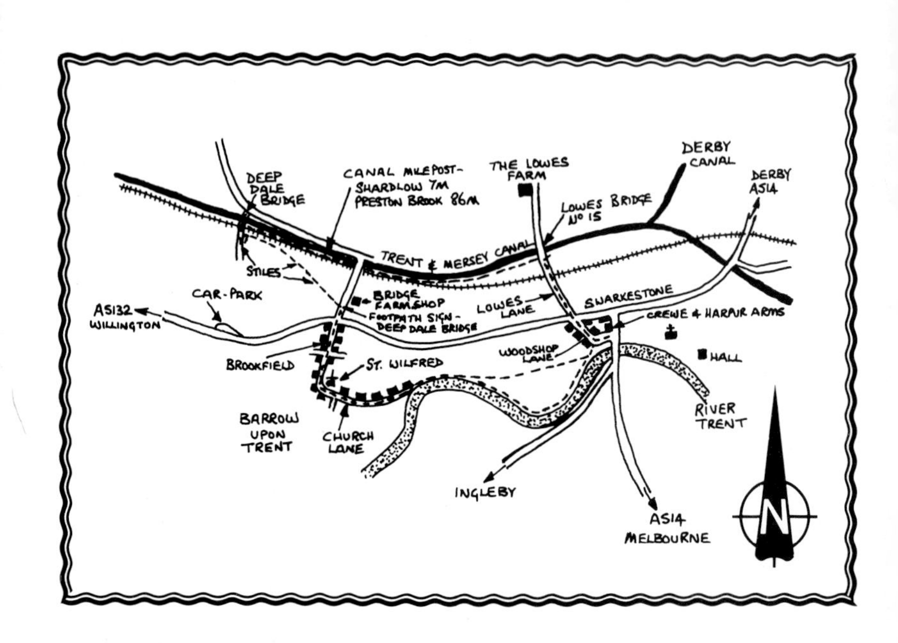

SWARKESTONE BRIDGE OVER RIVER TRENT

TRENT & MERSEY CANAL—WALK 4—
3½ miles—*allow 2 hours*

ROUTE—*Swarkestone—Lowes Bridge—Trent & Mersey Canal—Deep Dale Bridge —Barrow Upon Trent—River Trent—Swarkestone.*

MAPS—*1:50,000—Sheet No 128—Derby and Burton Upon Trent—1:25,000—Sheet SK 22/32—Burton Upon Trent*

CAR PARK—*no official one in Swarkestone. Parking space beside Lowes Lane, near canal. Lay-by car park on A5132 just west of Barrow Upon Trent, Grid Ref: SK348286.*

ABOUT THE WALK—From Swarkestone you follow a lane to the Trent & Mersey Canal, which you then follow for more than a mile to Deep Dale bridge. Here you cross the fields to the attractive village of Barrow Upon Trent. Here you first follow the river Trent before crossing the fields to Swarkestone and its impressive bridge over the Trent.

WALKING INSTRUCTIONS—From Swarkestone follow Woodshop Lane through the village past Crows Nest and path sign—Barrow on Trent—on your left (you will be entering Swarkestone from there). Cross the A5132 road and continue ahead along Lowes Lane, Cross the railway line and, just at the bridge (No 15) over the canal,turn right and gain the tow path. Turn left under the bridge and follow the tow path for just over a mile. After ½ mile pass under a road bridge with the road running along the righthandside of the canal. At the next bridge—Deep Dale Bridge—ascend to it via the path on the otherside of it. Turn right and cross the bridge over the railway line and turn left at the stile and descend the steps bearing left. Just before the railway track turn right and keep the field boundary on your left to the next stile. Over this bear right across the field to the next stile and keep the hedge on your left to the following stile.Cross the subsequent field to the minor road, with stile and path sign—Deepdale Bridge and Sinfin. Opposite is the Bridge Farm shop.

Turn right to the A5132 road. Cross over and walk along Brookfield into Barrow Upon Trent. Keep straight ahead into Church Lane and follow it past St. Wilfred's church and round to your left to approach the river Trent. At the end of the lane is the stile and footpath sign. First along a hedged path before a footbridge. Keep to the banksides for the next field before bearing left diagonally across it to the righthandside of a small plantation. The pathline keeps close to the field boundary for four fields to Meadow Farm and the path sign you saw at the beginning in Swarkestone. This path is not used often, and the fisherman's path along the bankside to Meadow Farm may be easier to follow. Entering Swarkestone onto Woodshop Lane turn right to see the bridge with Crewe & Harpur Arms on your left, beside the A514 road.

SWARKESTONE—famed for its bridges; the five arched bridge over the Trent dates from 1796, the remainder almost a mile long dates back to the 14th century. In 1643 Sir John Gell, the Parliamentary Governor of Derbyshire, routed the Cavaliers. In 1745 the advance guard of Charles Stuart reached here—their most southern point. Close by are the remains of an Elizabethan hall built by Sir Richard Harpur and designed by John Smithson who was deeply involved in Bolsover Castle. The church has many monuments to the Harpur family.

Some Canal Features To Look For

STOP PLANKS—in various places can be seen vertical grooves in the canal wall with handled planks stacked nearby. The planks were slotted into the grooves sealing the canal while repairs or cleaning of drained section was carried out.

ROPE GROOVES—on the side of bridges, sometimes with cast iron shields, can be seen the grooves cut by the horse tow lines over the decades, such as on the Beeston Canal.

TURNOVER BRIDGES—in a few places where the towpath switches sides of the canal a bridge was built to enable the horse to cross over without unhitching the line. See the Nottingham canal, beyond the Museum near the Trent. The remains of a horse bridge can be seen near Bullbridge on the Cromford Canal.

SWING BRIDGES—as the name implies the bridge could be swung out of the way to allow boats to pass. See the swing bridge at the High Peak Junction on the Cromford Canal.

FLAT-DECKED BRIDGES—in mining areas or places where subsidence is likely to occur, simple bridges were made that could be jacked up.

SKEW BRIDGES—most canal bridges are built at right angles to the canal. In a few cases to avoid the Z bend in the road the bridge was built at an angle.

BASIC LOCK FEATURES—

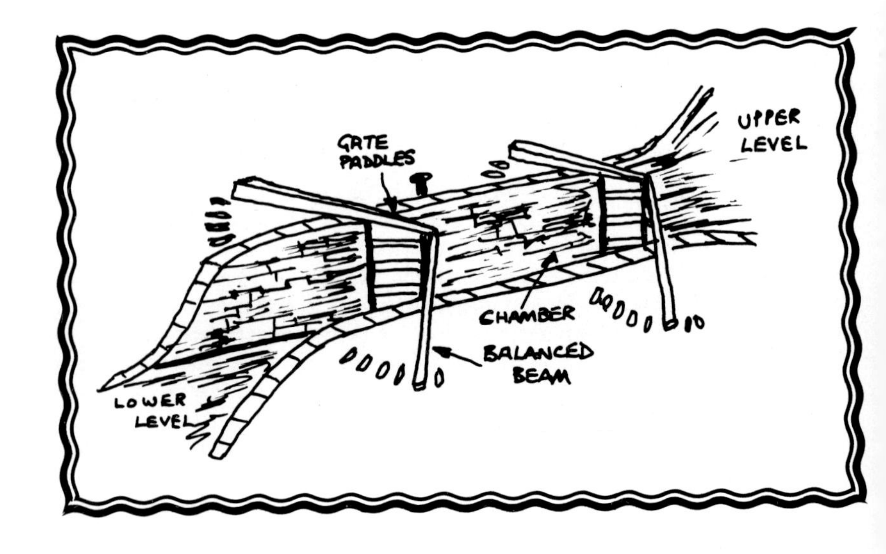

CANAL MUSEUMS

1. Nottingham Canal Museum,
   Canal Street,
   Nottingham. Tel. Nottingham (0602)—284602

2. Plus Pleasures Marine,
   Clock Warehouse,
   London Road,
   Shardlow,
   Derby. Tel. Derby (0332) 792844

3. The Leawood Pumphouse,
   The Cromford Canal Society Ltd.,
   Old Wharf,
   Mill Lane,
   Cromford,
   Matlock,
   Derbyshire. Tel. Wirksworth (062982—3727)

4. The National Waterways Museum,
   The Boat Museum,
   Dockyard Road,
   Ellesmere Port,
   South Wirral,
   L65 4EF Tel. 051-355 5017

OTHERS OF RELATED INTEREST—

1. The Erewash Museum,
   High Street,
   Ilkeston,
   Derbyshire.
   DE7 5SE Tel. Ilkeston (0602)—303361

2. The Bottle Kiln,
   West Hallam,
   Derbyshire
   DE7 6HP Tel. 0602—329442

3. Peak District Mining Museum,
   The Pavillion,
   South Parade,
   Matlock Bath,
   Derbyshire Tel. Matlock (0629)—3834

4. The Arkwright Society,
   Cromford Mill,
   Lea Road,
   Cromford,
   Derbyshire. Tel. Wirksworth 4305

5. Derby Industrial Museum,
   The Silk Mill,
   Off Full Street,
   Derby DE1 3AR.
   Tel. 31111 Ext. 740

CANAL SOCIETIES

Area Leisure Officer,
British Waterways Board,
24, Meadow Lane,
Nottingham. NG2 3HL

Chesterfield Canal Society,
Mrs C A Richardson,
15, Coral Drive,
Aughton,
Sheffield. S31 ORA

The Cromford Canal Society Ltd.,
Old Wharf,
Mill Lane,
Cromford,
Matlock,
Derbyshire.

The Erewash Canal Preseration & Development Association,
E G Harrison,
31, Derby Road,
Risley,
Derby,
DE7 3SY

Nottingham Canal Society,
B.Gerrard,
164, Charlbury Road,
Nottingham.

Trent & Mersey Canal Society,
M.D. Gray,
7, Cloverdale,
Weeping Cross,
Stafford.
ST17 4QJ

EASTWOOD LOCK, EREWASH CANAL

SUGGESTED FURTHER READING— *a random selection*

The Canals of the East Midlands Charles Hadfield *David & Charles*
The Canals of the West Midlands Charles Hadfield *David & Charles*
British Canals—an Illustrated History Charles Hadfield *David & Charles 1979*
James Brindley H.Bode *Shire Publications 1973*
The Trent & Mersey Canal Lindsay *David & Charles 1979*
The Nutbrook Canal P.Stevenson *David & Charles 1971*
The Erewash Canal—a cruising and walking guide *Erewash Canal Preservation and Development Association 1980*
Canal—Shardlow—Local History Trail No 18 *Arkwright Society 1981*
The Chesterfield Canal C.Richardson & J.C.Bird*Chesterfield Canal Society 1985*
Nicholson/Ordnance Survey Guide to the Waterways—Vol 2—Central
Nicholson/Ordnance Survey Guide to the Waterways—Vol 3—North

CANAL INN, BULLBRIDGE

FORTHCOMING CANAL WALK BOOKS—

BY JOHN N. MERRILL

Vol.2—Derbyshire, Staffordshire and Cheshire.
deals with—Macclesfield, Caldon, Trent & Mersey, Peak Forest and Ashton Canals.

Vol.3—Nottinghamshire, Leicestershire and Lincolnshire.
deals with—River Trent, Grantham Canal, River Soar, Witham Navigation, and Foss Dyke Navigation.

OTHER BOOKS BY JOHN N.MERRILL & PUBLISHED BY JNM PUBLICATIONS

DAY WALK GUIDES

PEAK DISTRICT: SHORT CIRCULAR WALKS Fifteen carefully selected walks—3 to 5 miles—starting from a car park. The walks cover the variety of the area—the gritstone edges, limestone dales, and peat moorland. All follow well defined paths; include a pub for lunch; and are suitable for all the family. 44 pages 16 maps 32 photographs ISBN 0 907496 16 4

PEAK DISTRICT TOWN WALKS Twelve short circular walks around the principal towns and villages of the Peak District. Including Castleton, Buxton, Hathersage, Eyam,Tissington and Ashbourne. Each walk has a detailed map and extensive historical notes complete with pictures. 60 pages 12 maps 96 photographs ISBN 0 907496 20 2

PEAK DISTRICT: LONG CIRCULAR WALKS Fifteen differing walks 12 to 18 miles long for the serious hiker. Many follow lesser used paths in the popular areas, giving a different perspective to familiar landmarks. 64 pages 16 maps 28 photographs ISBN 0 907496 17 2

WESTERN PEAKLAND—CIRCULAR WALKS The first book to cover this remarkably attractive side of the National Park—west of Buxton. The guide combines both long and short walks. 25 -3 to 11 mile long walks with extremely detailed maps to help you explore the area. 48 pages 23 maps 22 photographs ISBN 0 907496 15 6

12 SHORT CIRCULAR WALKS AROUND MATLOCK 12 walks of about 4 miles long into the Matlock area rich in history and folklore and make ideal family outings. Included is an 'alpine' walk, using Matlock Bath's cable car as part of the route. 52 pages 44 photographs 12 maps ISBN 0 907496 25 3

SHORT CIRCULAR WALKS IN THE DUKERIES More than 25 walks in the Nottinghamshire/Sherwood Forest area, past many of the historic buildings that make up the Dukeries area. ISBN 0 907496 29 6

DERBYSHIRE AND THE PEAK DISTRICT CANAL WALKS More than 20 walks both short and long along the canals in the area—Cromford, Erewash, Chesterfield, Derby, Trent, Peak Forest and Macclesfield canals. ISBN 0 907496 30 X

HIKE TO BE FIT: STROLLING WITH JOHN John Merrill's personal guide to walking in the countryside to keep fit and healthy. He describes what equipment to use, where to go, how to map read, use a compass and what to do about blisters! 36 pages 23 photos 2 sketches 3 charts ISBN 0 907496 19 9

CHALLENGE WALKS

JOHN MERRILL'S PEAK DISTRICT CHALLENGE WALK A 25 mile circular walk from Bakewell, across valleys and heights involving 3,700 feet of ascent. More than 2,000 people have already completed the walk. A badge and completion certificate is available to those who complete. 32 pages 18 photographs 9 maps ISBN 0 907496 18 0

JOHN MERRILL'S YORKSHIRE DALES CHALLENGE WALK A 23 mile circular walk from Kettlewell in the heart of the Dales. The route combines mountain, moorlands, limestone country and dale walking with 3,600 feet of ascent. A badge and certificate is available to those who complete the route. 32 pages 16 photographs 8 maps ISBN 0 907196 28 8

THE RIVER'S WAY A two day walk of 43 miles, down the length of the Peak District National Park. Inaugurated and created by John, the walk starts at Edale, the end of the Pennine Way, and ends at Ilam. Numerous hostels, campgrounds, B&B, and pubs lie on the route, as you follow the five main river systems of the Peak—Noe, Derwent, Wye, Dove, and Manifold. 52 pages 35 photographs 7 maps ISBN 0 907496 08 3

PEAK DISTRICT: HIGH LEVEL ROUTE A hard 90 mile, weeks walk, around the Peak District, starting from Matlock. As the title implies the walk keeps to high ground while illustrating the dramatic landscape of the Peak District.The walk was inaugurated and created by John and is used by him for training for his major walks! 60 pages 31 photographs 13 maps ISBN 0 907496 10 5

PEAK DISTRICT MARATHONS The first reference book to gather together all the major and classical long walks of the Peak District between 25 and 50 miles long. Many are challenge walks with badges and completion cards for those who complete. The longest walk—280 miles —inaugurated by John is around the entire Derbyshire boundary. Each walk has a general map, accommodation list, and details of what guides and maps are needed. 56 pages 20 photographs 20 maps ISBN 0 907496 13 X

HISTORICAL GUIDES

WINSTER—A VISITOR'S GUIDE A detailed look at a former lead mining community which still retains a Morris dancing team and annual pancake races. A two mile walk brings you to many historical buildings including the 17th century Market House. Illustrated by old photographs. 20 pages 21 photographs 1 map ISBN 0 907496 21 0

DERBYSHIRE INNS The first book to tell the story behind more than 150 inns in the Peak District and Derbyshire area. With details of legends, murders and historical anecdotes, the book gives added pleasure or impetus to explore the pubs of the region. Profusely illustrated with 65 photographs and a brief history of brewing in Derbyshire. 68 pages 57 photographs 5 maps ISBN 0 907496 11 3

100 HALLS AND CASTLES OF THE PEAK DISTRICT AND DERBYSHIRE A visitor's guide to the principal historical buildings of the region. Many are open to the public and the guide describes the history of the building from the Domesday Book to the present time.The book is illustrated by 120 photographs and makes an excellent souvenir gift of one of England's finest architectural areas. 120 pages 116 photographs 4 maps ISBN 0 907496 23 7

TOURING THE PEAK DISTRICT AND DERBYSHIRE Twenty circular routes of about 50 miles for the motorist or cyclist. Each route has a set theme, such as the gritstone edges or in the steps of Mary, Queen of Scots. Deatiled maps for each route and fifty photographs make this a useful companion to the Peak District/Derbyshire area. 76 pages 45 photographs 20 maps ISBN 0 907496 22 9

JOHN'S MARATHON WALKS

EMERALD COAST WALK The story of John's walk up the total length of the west coast of Ireland and exploration of more than fifty islands—1,600 miles. 132 pages 32 photographs 12 maps ISBN 0 907496 02 4

TURN RIGHT AT LAND'S END In 1978 John Merrill became the first person to walk the entire coastline of Britain—6,824 miles in ten months. The book details the route, how he ascended our three major mountains and how he found a wife. Included are more than 200 photographs he took on the walk, which is also a unique guide to our coastline. 246 pages 214 photographs 10 maps ISBN 0 907496 24 5

WITH MUSTARD ON MY BACK John has gathered together the stories of his first decade of walking—1970-1980. Here is a collection of unique walks in Britain, from a 2,000 mile walk linking the ten National Parks of England and Wales together to a 450 mile walk from Norwich to Durham. ISBN 0 907496 27 X

TURN RIGHT AT DEATH VALLEY During the summer of 1984, John walked coast to coast across America, a distance of 4,226 miles in 177 days. Few have walked across and none have taken so difficult a route. He crossed all the main mountain ranges, climbed 14,000 foot mountains, crossed deserts in 100 degrees, walked rim to rim of the Grand Canyon in 8½ hours, and crossed the famed Death Valley. The walk is without parallel and the story is the remarkable tale of this unique adventure. ISBN 0 907496 26 1

WALK RECORD CHART

Date walked

CHESTERFIELD CANAL ....
WALK 1—*SPINKHILL—5 miles* ....
WALK 2—*KILLAMARSH—4 miles* ....
WALK 3—*THORPE SALVIN—3 miles* ....
WALK 4—*WORKSOP—4 miles* ....
WALK 5—*WORKSOP—6 miles* ....
WALK 6—*RANBY—5 miles* ....
WALK 7—*RETFORD—5½ miles* ....
WALK 8—*MISTERTON—3½ miles* ....
WALK 9—*WORKSOP—26 miles* ....
CROMFORD CANAL ....
WALK 1—*CROMFORD—3 miles* ....
WALK 2—*CROMFORD—7 miles* ....
WALK 3—*WHATSTANDWELL—7 miles* ....
EREWASH CANAL ....
WALK 1—*SHIPLEY PARK—6 miles* ....
WALK 2—*COSSALL—3 miles* ....
WALK 3—*COSSALL—9½ miles* ....
WALK 4—*SANDIACRE—3 miles* ....
WALK 5—*SANDIACRE—4 miles* ....
WALK 6—*TRENTLOCK—6 miles* ....
WALK 7—*END TO END—11½ miles* ....
NUTBROOK CANAL ....
WALK 1—*STANTON BY DALE—7 miles* ....
DERBY CANAL ....
WALK 1—*LONG EATON—9 miles* ....
WALK 2—*SWARKESTONE—3½ miles* ....
BEESTON CANAL ....
WALK 1—*ATTENBOROUGH—4½ miles* ....
WALK 2—*BEESTON LOCK—3 miles* ....
WALK 3—*NOTTINGHAM—4½ miles* ....
NOTTINGHAM CANAL ....
WALK 1—*NOTTINGHAM—3 miles* ....
TRENT & MERSEY CANAL ....
WALK 1—*TRENTLOCK—3 miles* ....
WALK 2—*SHARDLOW—3 miles* ....
WALK 3—*SHARDLOW—5 miles* ....
WALK 4—*SWARKESTONE—3½ miles* ....

BENNERLEY VIADUCT

EQUIPMENT NOTES
—some personal thoughts

BOOTS—perferably with a leather upper, of medium weight, with a vibram sole. I always add a foam cushioned insole to help cushion the base of my feet.

SOCKS—I generally wear two thick pairs as this helps to minimise blisters. The inner pair of loop stitch variety and approximately 80% wool. The outer a thick rib pair of approximately 80% wool.

WATERPROOFS—for general walking I wear a T shirt or shirt with a cotton wind jacket on top. You generate heat as you walk and I prefer to layer my clothes to avoid getting too hot. Depending on the season will dictate how many layers you wear. In soft rain I just use my wind jacket for I know it quickly dries out. In heavy downpours I slip on a neoprene lined cagoule, and although hot and clammy it does keep me reasonably dry. Only in extreme conditions will I don overtrousers, much preferring to get wet and feel comfortable.

FOOD—as I walk I carry bars of chocolate, for they provide instant energy and are light to carry. In winter a flask of hot coffee is welcome. I never carry water and find no hardship from doing so, but this is a personal matter.From experience I find the more I drink the more I want. You should always carry some extra food such as Kendal Mint Cake for emergencies.

RUCKSACK—for day walking I use a climbing rucksac of about 40 litre capacity and although excess space it does mean that the sac is well padded and with a shoulder strap. Inside apart from the basics for the day I carry gloves, balaclava, spare pullover and a pair of socks.

MAP & COMPASS—when I am walking I always have the relevant map—usually 1:25,000 scale—open in my hand. This enables me to constantly check that I am walking the right way. In case of bad weather I carry a Silva type compass, which once mastered gives you complete confidence in thick cloud or mist.

DERWENT HOTEL, WHATSTANDWELL

JOHN MERRILL'S CANAL WALKING BADGE

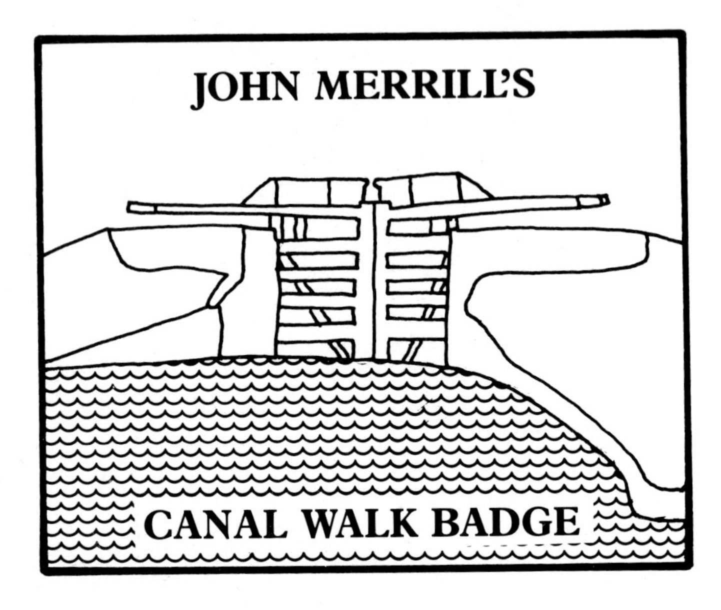

JOHN MERRILL'S CANAL WALKING BADGE

Walk six or more of the walks in this book and send details to John Merrill at JNM Publications, enlosing £1.75, for a special four colour embroidered badge.

START OF DERBY CANAL—SANDIACRE END

NAVIGATION INN, DERBY CANAL

DERBY CANAL BRIDGE

REMEMBER AND OBSERVE THE COUNTRY CODE

ENJOY THE COUNTRYSIDE AND RESPECT ITS LIFE AND WORK.

GUARD AGAINST ALL RISK OF FIRE.

FASTEN ALL GATES.

KEEP YOUR DOGS UNDER CLOSE CONTROL.

KEEP TO PUBLIC PATHS ACROSS FARMLAND.

USE GATES AND STILES TO CROSS FENCES, HEDGES AND WALLS.

LEAVE LIVESTOCK, CROPS AND MACHINERY ALONE.

TAKE YOUR LITTER HOME—PACK IT IN, PACK IT OUT.

HELP TO KEEP ALL WATER CLEAN.

PROTECT WILDLIFE, PLANTS AND TREES.

TAKE SPECIAL CARE ON COUNTRY ROADS.

MAKE NO UNNECESSARY NOISE.

TRENT & MERSEY CANAL MILEPOST